# ADVANCE PRAISE

How we estimate ourselves is in direct proportion to how successful we are in life. Often, we view ourselves as to how others perceive us. This limits our capabilities. Being positive in our ability to do what we want and achieve our goals is very important. This book aims to achieve that objective, and I consider it a must-read. I commend the writer on a well-written book.

**Gul Mirpuri,** *Founder Chairman, The Indian Businessmen's Association, Hong Kong*

Self-esteem and confidence can be powerful tools to shape our destiny. In a time of social media and instant gratification, our self-esteem can take a major hit if we view everything we do or achieve through this lens. Shobha Nihalani's book, *Self-Esteem in a Selfie World*, takes an in-depth look at what constitutes our self-esteem or lack thereof but in an interesting, easy-to-read style. Interspersed with real-life examples, she brings out the subtle nuances that can help us all reboot! A must-read!!

**Dr. Harry S. Banga,** *Founder, Chairman and CEO, The Caravel Group Ltd*

*Self-Esteem in a Selfie World* is an important book for our time. It speaks to all of us who are overwhelmed with messaging from everywhere, all the time. It makes the case that we need to find ways to pause to refuel ourselves and to protect our self-esteem. It is both an enjoyable and educational read.

**Shalini Mahtani,** *MBE,*
*Founder and CEO, The Zubin Foundation*

In this informative and thought-provoking book, Shobha has done a wonderful job in exploring how healthy self-esteem, self-acceptance and persistence can have so many positive influences in our lives and lead us to different ways of success. Her thesis is substantiated with many real-life stories which make her book a most refreshingly interesting read.

**Anderson Chow Ka-ming,** *Hong Kong*

*Self-Esteem in a Selfie World* is insightful and creates awareness of what is relevant in each one of us to thrive in this complicated world. The book shares modern-day experiences, from corporate to personal, offering us a deeper understanding of how self-esteem can affect every decision we make in life. A must-read for all age groups.

**Deepak Ohri,** *CEO, Lebua Hotels & Resorts*

This book addresses the dilemma of people who get easily trapped by weaving a net of untrue and un-useful conclusions. Written in a very easy-to-grasp style along with crystal clear relevant case stories, it triggers soul-searching experiences to feel stronger and melt away the self-imposed limitations. Very engaging and enlightening, author Shobha has done elaborate research and imparts practical ideas to live life with elegance and respect. We can say it is a user's manual for living a life worth it!

**Siri and Sat Khalsa,** *Creators of*
*InnerMost Shift Coaching Model*

# SELF-ESTEEM IN A SELFIE WORLD

SHOBHA NIHALANI

# SELF-ESTEEM IN A SELFIE WORLD

## Sculpting the True You

SHOBHA NIHALANI

SELF-ESTEEM IN A SELFIE WORLD
Copyright © 2023 Shobha Nihalani
First published in 2023

Print: 978-1-76124-076-8
E-book: 978-1-76124-044-7
Hardback: 978-1-76124-043-0

All rights reserved. No part of this book may be reproduced, stored in a retrieval system, or transmitted by any means (electronic, mechanical, photocopying, recording, or otherwise) without written permission from the author.

Because of the dynamic nature of the Internet, any web addresses or links contained in this book may have changed since publication and may no longer be valid. The information in this book is based on the author's experiences and opinions. The views expressed in this book are solely those of the author and do not necessarily reflect the views of the publisher; the publisher hereby disclaims any responsibility for them.

The author of this book does not dispense any form of medical, legal, financial, or technical advice either directly or indirectly. The intent of the author is solely to provide information of a general nature to help you in your quest for personal development and growth. In the event you use any of the information in this book, the author and the publisher assume no responsibility for your actions. If any form of expert assistance is required, the services of a competent professional should be sought.

**Publishing information**
Publishing and design facilitated by Passionpreneur Publishing
A division of Passionpreneur Organization Pty Ltd
ABN: 48640637529

Melbourne, VIC | Australia
www.PassionpreneurPublishing.com

To all those who have the courage to stand up for themselves, and more so, to those who endure in silence.

# CONTENTS

| | |
|---|---|
| *Foreword* by Anand Neelakantan | ix |
| *Foreword* by Krishna Kumari | xiii |
| *Acknowledgements* | xv |
| *Preface* | xvii |
| | |
| **PART 1: REBOOT: SENSORY INPUTS** | **1** |
| Chapter 1: Force of Nature | 3 |
| Chapter 2: Look at Yourself Respectfully | 27 |
| Chapter 3: Imposter Syndrome | 51 |
| | |
| **PART 2: REFLECT: BODY MIND HEART** | **75** |
| Chapter 4: Big Talk Small Talk | 77 |
| Chapter 5: Toxic Workplace | 99 |
| Chapter 6: Social Media Trap | 125 |
| | |
| **PART 3: REVAMP: MINDSET MATTERS** | **149** |
| Chapter 7: Fears of Being Unique: Society and Culture | 151 |
| Chapter 8: Know Thyself: Handling Identity Crisis | 175 |
| Chapter 9: Awareness through Self-compassion | 195 |
| | |
| *About the Author* | 219 |

# FOREWORD

*Aham Brahmasmi*—I am the universal consciousness, I am the whole—forms the basis of ancient Indian thought. No culture would have taught humans to love oneself more than the Indian culture. When many religions talked about humans being the children of sin, the Vedas proclaimed *Twam Amritasya Putra*, you children of immortality. The thought that life and death are cyclical and eternal stems from this love for self.

In 1818, Max Müller, the doyen of Indophiles, wrote a book named *India: What Can It Teach Us?* In it, he claimed Indians are not active, acquisitive and aggressive, but are spiritual, passive, meditative and reflective. This laid the foundation of the belief that India is a spiritual civilization. Nothing could be farther from the truth. There has never been a civilization that celebrated life in all its myriad beauty and forms like India. Some mendicants left everything and sought the solitude of the mountain caves to reflect on life, but they were just a handful. The majority sought bliss in everyday life. *Artha*, acquiring wealth, and *Kama*, following passion, became the two of four pillars that gave meaning to life—*Purushartha*. The other two pillars are *Dharma*, the code of ethics as defined by one's own conscience, and *Moksha*, the power to keep oneself detached from life while enjoying it. Whether one chooses the path of a mendicant and chooses to deny life in search of the self or chooses the way of the householder and seeks harmony in life, by pursuing the *Dharma*, *Artha*, *Kama* and *Moksha* ideals, what was at the centre was one's own self. In short, life was always about loving oneself. Every other love or passion or pursuit sprouted from this love of self.

Science and technology have brought us many blessings. They have also resulted in universalizing many problems. By the end of the last century, with the collapse of the Soviet Union, capitalism declared its triumph as the universal religion. The world became one massive trading place, connected through the Internet and in the past one and a half-decade, through social media. Capitalism works on discontentment. Without feeding a constant sense of dissatisfaction, it is impossible to make people buy more things. There is nothing wrong with discontentment per se. If the cavemen were contented, we would be still living in caves. Science is a product of discontent. If the speed that our feet could provide us was enough, we would not have invented wheels. If the hooves of horses could take us as fast as we wished, there would not have been any need for automobiles. It is our discontentment with the limitations that nature imposed on us which made us expand our limits. It is discontentment that fires the rockets and spaceship that would take us beyond the frontiers of the solar system and even the Milky Way to the edges of the universe. In a collective level, discontentment serves as the engine of progress.

As science progresses, we are bound to feel more and more discontented. This could be a virtuous cycle for the society, but for the individual, this could mean disastrous. Every moment of life, we are bombarded with cues that make us feel we lack something in life. Not a single moment passes without being distracted by a chime on our mobile phone. We find at least one of our friends are vacationing in an exotic location, another has brought a luxurious SUV, some have the latest version of the costly phone, another has designer clothes and so on. When we look around, what are we seeing?

Our cramped apartment is piled with dirty laundry. Our phone is chiming with the tenth reminder from an irritated boss about the completion of an impossible assignment. A grumpy overweight spouse is plonked on the sofa, glued to the mobile. The cranky children are yelling for constant attention. Why is our life so drab and dreadful when everyone else in the world seems to have a fantastic time? Why all my 5,000 friends on Facebook look like models out of a fashion magazine when I look like the unfortunate *vada pav* that fell on the floor of a crowded Mumbai local? The reason for your friend to look like a fashion model may lie with the filters on his/her mobile phone. Life does not have such filters that spray a golden hue on everything.

The irony is that everyone feels the same sense of inadequacy. We forget that social media does not capture the entire life of anyone, but the best snippet in one's life. The photo of our friend vacationing in Seychelles does not tell the tale of their slogging for next three years to pay the EMI of this vacation or the fact that it was their only vacation in 10 years. When we have 5,000 friends on Facebook, statistically, a few scores of them will be having a great time at any given moment. An equal number will be having some horrible things happening and the majority would be living everyday life. But we see only the first group and every moment, we are fed with such images. Discontentment is good if we get time to work on achieving our goal. If our real-life friend performs something great, it fills us with happiness for we know the trials and tribulation he/she has undertaken to achieve it. If we are discontented that we have not achieved what we want, such successes inspire us to work harder and reach our goal. When we are continuously fed the success stories through social media of people who we barely know, we have no time even to recover from the assault or to be inspired by it. It fills us with numbness, with a sense of self-loathing and inadequacy.

What Shobha Nihalani has done in this beautiful book is to give us tools to overcome this sense of inadequacy that is threatening to overwhelm us. Through carefully crafted chapters, she helps us to rediscover our self-worth and live life with a purpose and harmony.

**Anand Neelakantan**
Novelist, Screenwriter, Public speaker,
Columnist and Television personality

# FOREWORD

I am very happy that my dear friend Mrs Shobha Nihalani is bringing out a book so aptly titled *Self-esteem in a Selfie World*.

Her book deals with issues that affect many people in our so-called virtual world, particularly youngsters, who have been exposed to the digital world and find themselves misfits in the real world. I remember our beloved guru, Dada J. P. Vaswani, telling us that we live in an era of communication revolution, but many of us are getting more and more disconnected from real people and the real world.

The truth of the matter is our self-esteem, our self-confidence, indeed, our destiny is in our own hands. Rev. Dada told us, 'We are sowing seeds every day, every hour, every moment in the field of life. Every thought I think, every word I utter, every deed I perform, every emotion, every feeling, every wish that awakens within me—these are all seeds that I am sowing in the field of my life. In course of time, these seeds will germinate and bear fruit. Bitter or sweet they may be—but I shall have to eat those fruits. No one else can eat them for me....'

Dada taught us that we are the architects of our own destiny, the builders of our own fate. The moment we become aware that our destiny is created by our own thoughts, words, actions and desires, then there is always the possibility that is open to us, to correct and improve ourselves.

God endowed each and every one of us with a free will, and each of us has the freedom to change our destiny at every step, in every round of life. In other words, each of us has the freedom of choice to act—to choose right or wrong. At every step of life, we can make the effort to improve our condition. Through our actions, we can actually succeed in changing our own karma and, thus, altering our own destiny.

Is this not true empowerment? Is this not reboot, reflect and revive in essence?

'When writing the story of your life, don't let anyone else hold the pen', a wise man told us. Every thought you think, every word you speak and every act you perform are adding up to the story of your life.

That is exactly what this beautiful book urges us to do: to take charge of your life, to make your life meaningful, purposeful, worthwhile, useful to yourself and others and, above all, joyous and peaceful, so that you will wake up every morning fresh as the proverbial morning rose—newly washed in dew and eager to spread your fragrance all around.

Wake up to reality; wake up to the real world around you. Stay connected to the Source. Stay connected to the true self within.

**Krishna Kumari**
Working Chairperson,
Sadhu Vaswani Mission, Pune

# ACKNOWLEDGEMENTS

This book would not have been possible without the insights of experts and the many people who willingly shared their self-esteem stories. Thank you.

Many of their personal experiences were traumatic. In all of these heartfelt stories is the spirit of courage to face the inner pain, learn, and transform.

In the process of understanding the vast topic of self-esteem from a scientific perspective, I followed an intense routine of reading. I researched a vast array of case studies, journals, reviewed papers, columns, magazines, and self-help books. As much as I gleaned the science, I also understood from experiential learning. Low self-esteem has affected almost everyone on this planet. I have done my best to put together all the recent issues in our selfie world that knocks down our self-esteem. I continue on this path of self-development and will continue to share my learnings with the world.

I would like to express my sincere appreciation to Andrew Donlan PhD, for his in-depth suggestions and professional editing.

I am deeply grateful to a wonderful soul Gautam Ganglani, author of Breaking Bread. He introduced me to the dynamic entrepreneur, coach, speaker, and award-winning author, also known as 'Mr Passion' - Moustafa Hamwi of Passionpreneur Publishing. Thank you for inspiring me to see a wider perspective of my book.

Project Manager Cat Martindale-Vale has been an ideal motivator and guide. She made the publishing process easy and rewarding.

To my family, friends and well-wishers, I am grateful for your constant support and feedback.

# PREFACE

Nothing is more important than the judgement we pass on ourselves. How we esteem ourselves touches the very core of our existence. Self-esteem is one of the most integral ingredients for a fulfilling life. It essentially refers to the way we view our own selves—good or bad—as well as our ability to accept who we are, as we are.

Self-esteem is a vitally important psychological strength to adapt to a constantly evolving world that is dismayingly unpredictable and turbulent.

In our modern age, we find the reality of life increasingly shrouded by the curtain of digital illusions. The digital communications revolution—the internet, social media, smartphones, online dating apps and so much more—has transformed society and, indeed, how we experience reality itself. Many of us have the habit of using these platforms for multiple hours a day, in some instances, even to the point of addiction. As a result, we are constantly assaulted by the countless messages that we see online, which, in turn, leads us to curate the parts of our lives that we choose to share to control how other users see us. As others also do so, we are presented with almost unavoidable social comparisons. These habits, day in and day out, can easily impinge on our very sense of self. One doesn't need to be an expert to see that social media platforms have become worlds where we live out virtual lives, lives where we feel bound to amass likes and comments in order to boost our increasingly fragile self-esteem. This 'social currency' infiltrates our deepest sense of who we are. In many cases, social media is capable of deconstructing our thinking and undermining our self-perception. Before long, it can turn the self-assured into self-doubter.

We are influenced by the news through our non-stop electronic habits. This continuous exposure to passive input creates an impression on our minds. How we esteem the person that we are is directly and indirectly affected by what we see on media platforms and how we relate to people in our lives. The constant updates—many of which project an illusion that people live fairy-tale lives—lead to feeling that something is amiss in one's own life.

Our thoughts have the power to influence our decisions and actions in ways that are essentially life changing. Our way of thinking is so powerful that we can create our own heaven or hell. The Mahabharata is an ancient Indian epic, where the main story revolves around two branches of a family who, in the Kurukshetra War, fight for the throne of Hastinapura. Many believe that there are symbolic messages that are being conveyed through these texts. One is the idea of our inner battle to struggle amid our imperfect human condition. How we take charge of our inner life and direct our thoughts are fundamentally dependent on how we view ourselves as individuals through the lens of others.

A mindfulness teacher explained that social media is like a slot machine. We keep checking our feeds chasing after the expected dopamine fix. This hit of pleasure may happen once, but after it passes, we are left with the discomforting dismay at something is missing within ourselves and our lives. Even after we log off, an echo of the abrasive voice lingers.

We assume that as adults we will be well adjusted and capable of achieving goals and facing problems skilfully. But conflicting emotions and thoughts may throw us off track and before we know it, this inner voice is taking over our lives. Self-esteem is a critical tool here, for it strengthens us in the face of challenges.

To have high self-esteem is not the same as being arrogant or self-absorbed, but rather being aware of one's positives and capable of accepting any negatives with compassion and a certain amount of inner strength. A person with self-esteem is someone able to stand firm in the face of criticism. A person with low self-esteem is someone ceaselessly battered by an internal voice that says they are 'not good enough', 'incapable and stupid', 'failing in relationships,' 'undeserving of promotions' or 'an imposter'. Such internal talk undermines the self.

Eventually, the bitter tortured individual reaches the brink of a psychological break, praying for an answer. Yes, praying. That's when realization hits that the critical voice has been creating the chaos within. Not everybody practises prayer, and I respect that. I can only invite readers to keep an open mind. My own experience leaves me with no choice but to conclude that prayer can in fact help to detach from this voice and this feeling of self-deprecation. Spirituality is a broad concept; it is not just a search for the meaning of life but also a lifelong quest to pursue self-knowledge and wellness.

To me, healthy self-esteem gives the feeling of standing on solid ground, sturdy, unshakeable, never trembling in the face of challenges. Losing one's self-esteem feels off-kilter, as if the ground cracks open and we are swallowed into an abyss, unable to shift out of that self-doubt.

I believe that a person with strong self-belief and a resilient attitude can achieve their full potential. Quite simply, if people feel better about themselves, they perform better. Self-esteem is, therefore, an ability to see one's own flaws objectively and work towards a positive change through self-awareness. This is the starting point.

In every chapter, I shall attempt to go deeper into self-esteem to understand how we think and behave and why we don't quite accomplish what we set out to achieve.

I make no pretence here of being an expert in the field of psychology. I have no advanced degrees nor can I promise that my views are a perfect compendium of current thinking. What I can say, however, is that my views about self-esteem are the result of a lifelong quest. As a result, I have looked deeply within my own experience and have read extensively on the topic. Over a broad span of time, experts have plumbed the depths of this topic through experiments and studies of all manner and form. Most agree that self-esteem does play a profound role in our lives.

I believe, intuitively, that a lot of our hopes and dreams die if we lack self-esteem. During my teenage years, I was influenced by many internal and external factors that affected my self-perception. Looking back, I can see in retrospect how many life decisions were made based on fear and a basic lack of trust within.

Over time, I have become aware of this internal voice. It still squeaks out its negativity and fear, telling me I am bound to fail. I have developed the ability to push back and change its tone. I have talked it down and made it milder. This has diminished its influence and allowed me to focus on my goals.

It took half a lifetime to understand that my own thoughts were undermining my interests, that my feelings towards myself were not friendly. I write in part to understand this very important fact that we are who we are through the lens of our life experiences and how we respond affects our own potential. As much as it might sound cliché to today's cynics, we must recognize that we are good enough.

We live in a world where life seems to change at breakneck pace. Everything seems ephemeral, as though the familiar reassurances of today might just soon disappear. We live by rushed schedules, fast food and instant coffee. We want to feel empowered and create lives full of meaning, but instead, we often scramble just to meet our basic needs. Technology permeates our lives 24/7. The benefits of modern life are clear, but we forget the toll it takes on our spirit. As a result, our inner life is a daily roller coaster. Instead of recognizing that it is our courage and persistence that define who we are, we are too prone to judge ourselves (and sometimes others) harshly. We have to admit that confusion and anxiety of life require us to revisit how we see others and the world. We need to remain grounded and begin anew. We need to check in with our inner selves from time to time. We need to reboot our assumptions, attitudes and lives.

# CHAPTER 1

# FORCE OF NATURE

*To trust one's mind and to know that one is worthy of happiness is the essence of self-esteem.*

—Nathaniel Branden

Life is not always a dream, it can have nightmarish moments, but some people know how to turn nightmares into dreams.

We know very well that successful people don't achieve greatness simply with a snap of their fingers or by wishing upon a star. The hardships they face can be unimaginably difficult. Whether someone is overcoming a disability or being born into poverty, they are tapping into a fire within to confront the obstacle head-on. Where does this determination come from, and why do some people seem to have it and others don't? In short, it stems from a sense of faith in oneself and one's ultimate goals. It is more than the so-called efficacy, which is confidence in one's abilities. When we have healthy self-esteem, we have a clear view not only of our own good traits but also our bad ones. We accept our weaknesses and vices along with our positive qualities; it is how we esteem ourselves. Do we have what it takes to be who we want to be in this world? The answer lies in our self-esteem.

In a nutshell, therefore, self-esteem is your opinion of yourself and your abilities. Depending on your circumstances, it can be high, low or somewhere in between. While it is normal to occasionally have doubts about ourselves, persistent and acute low self-esteem can be a problem, for it can leave us feeling insecure and unmotivated. Low self-esteemers might still be self-confident in certain areas of their life but not others.

According to some psychologists, self-esteem is the ultimate marker of psychological health [1].

This is clear when we see low self-esteemers approach life, work and relationships differently from those with healthy self-esteem.

The force of our nature that ignites self-esteem is intriguing.

## PERSISTENCE PAYS

Johnny K. was a 30-year-old tall, good-looking man with an unbeatable, optimistic attitude. He talked like he was an expert in his field, the film industry. Johnny had big plans to become a super successful filmmaker. He liked to boast about the 50-plus action-packed scripts he had written, and claimed his work was gold. Naturally, talk like that was criticized, and people laughed at him. Johnny's grandmother was one of the earliest actresses in Bollywood, the Indian film industry. She was quite a talented performer in her heyday. Johnny loved to share the story about his grandma's success and how he intended to make her proud. After all, it was her blood running through his veins.

But Johnny himself was an unknown entity in the industry, a novice. People scoffed at his arrogance. He had absolutely no knowledge of how to go about making a film. Yes, he had read many books on successful Hollywood filmmakers. Even though he had a college degree, he had little professional experience. He had worked in a few different companies but tended to defy authority. He was fired but would claim that he resigned because the job wasn't challenging enough. Johnny had never worked on film sets nor assisted any film directors in shoots.

Johnny's parents tried to talk him out of his wide-eyed idealism. They even told him that his grandmother died a pauper, with fame but no savings. Johnny's father, an engineer, wanted little to do with the film industry. He asked Johnny to join the family's lucrative mining business and was angered when Johnny rejected the offer. But Johnny didn't care. He had only one dream: to make a film. He asked his mother for funds, but she didn't want to antagonise his father. The family wouldn't invest in his madcap plan, so he turned to others. He contacted producers, pitched his story to actors and knocked on the doors of luminaries to seek help. But no one believed in him. Some offered kindly advice, while others told him to forget his dream. No producer wanted to invest in his film, which they thought was prohibitively expensive. Johnny offered to direct the film himself. The producers told him openly: 'Johnny your film needs a huge budget, you have no experience as a director, no actor will work with you, and no one will risk investing in an unknown filmmaker. Just give up.'

But Johnny was unshaken. He dismissed these naysayers as fools. As far as he was concerned, his film was going to be an action blockbuster and would lead to a franchise. Johnny never doubted his own abilities nor did he compromise his vision. Even if no one believed in him, he would remain steadfast.

Despite all these odds against him, he did it, he roped in a rising star as male lead. A film studio backed his request for an action choreographer from Hollywood. He acquired permission to film in a European country. He was finally able to make his big dream come true, a version of it only slightly less ambitious. But he did it. This year his action-packed film released to fantastic reviews.

Compare Johnny's storybook ending to the outcome of another individual with a similar dream. Manoj, who wanted to make a film, was rejected by two producers, criticized by a scriptwriter and told to get lost by a couple of studio heads. He gave up and took up an entry-level admin job [2].

Why do two people with the same dream have different attitudes to the same situation? The reason is that as unique individuals our default reactions to criticism are different from each other. Some people's self-esteem is more sensitive to difficulties and adversity.

A 19th-century psychologist and philosopher, William James called these areas 'contingencies of self-worth'. In his thinking, we make self-worth judgements based on specific ends or outcomes that we value. This is why a moral weakness that causes existential crisis in one person may be easily forgotten by another. It is why one person may feel devastated from a bad day at work, while someone else may laugh it off.

Each of us weighs differently how our daily experiences relate to our self-worth. These domains can include everything from appearance to competency, to family approval. It is in our nature to behave in certain ways, we are compelled in a direction based on who we are inherently.

Before we go further, William James also stated that there are three points that need to be understood about self-esteem.

- First, it is both a personality trait and a psychological state, which means it fluctuates often.
- Second, self-esteem is affected by success and failure.
- Third, it is dependent on the person's belief of what he/she must do to succeed or achieve his/her goals.

If self-esteem is dependent on the individual's motivation towards a goal, then the success or failure affects the self-esteem. It is a cycle of ups and downs.

To live a meaningful life, where we can enjoy our achievements and learn from our mistakes, our self-esteem must be firm and unconditional. We need to be willing to accept failure, especially in how it teaches us life lessons [3].

Self-esteem comes from how we answer the am I a good person or a bad person kind of questions and how we compare ourselves with others. The healthy self-esteem that comes from being a friend to oneself inspires us to reach goals. It motivates and energizes us to wake up, get to work and work damn hard.

## SPARK OF SUCCESS

Imagine if self-esteem is the spark that drives us forward and gives us energy to persist. Now imagine further that persistence is a force which in turn raises our self-esteem. This cyclical relationship or feedback loop between self-esteem and meaningful effort is an important point for psychiatrist and author, M. Scott Peck, who believes that the feeling of being valuable is the cornerstone of self-discipline [4].

We face many hardships in life that knock us down. A person with a fragile self-esteem may falter and give up. But if we have the right thinking and value ourselves, flaws and all, we will overcome our challenges. We will be able to do things that are meaningful, which in turn makes us more valuable to ourselves and the world around us. We persist and strive. Yet without adequate self-valuing, we don't pursue our goals; instead, we get stuck in a vicious cycle; we think we are not good enough and then we end up being uninspired to do anything meaningful. This, in turn, diminishes our self-worth. Thus, self-esteem and persistence nurture each other.

We all know of heroes who achieve amazing things through sheer inner grit. Have you ever wondered what mindset, attitude and thoughts make someone a high achiever? What inner resource enables them to overcome hardship, rejection and failure?

Born to a poor landless farmer in a small village of Appanaickenpatti Padur in Tamil Nadu, Arokiaswamy Velumani was so poor that he sought government subsidies to go through school and college. Velumani's father had given up on taking care of his wife and four children. He just couldn't endure the daily struggles to earn a wage anymore. Faced with her husband's helplessness, Velumani's mother took on the responsibility of keeping their head above water by investing in two buffaloes, the milk from which earned them a meagre ₹50 a week. But it managed to sustain the family for almost a decade.

Velumani kept up his studies and finally decided to start his career as a shift chemist at a small pharmaceutical company in Coimbatore. He earned ₹150 a month, less than a watchman. But he didn't complain. Every month he sent home a ₹100 and kept ₹50 for himself. This went on for four years until the capsule-making company collapsed, and Velumani found himself jobless. Undaunted, he managed to get a position at the government-run Bhabha Atomic Research Centre (BARC). There his salary was higher than he or his family had ever known—₹880.

Velumani spent 14 years at BARC, and for 10 of those years, he even had the opportunity to study for a doctorate in thyroid biochemistry. Velumani soon wanted to do something different. He had developed an idea which he believed would help make thyroid testing—prohibitively expensive for much of India's population—affordable. He wanted to use his expertise to set up special testing labs to detect thyroid disorders. Not only would this reach many thousands of people, but it would also be a huge moneymaking opportunity. Yet it was a risky venture. By then, he had a wife and two children, and quitting his job at BARC meant giving up a stable government salary. But in 1995, the day came when he felt he must follow his conviction. He handed in his resignation letter, came home and told his wife. Although it must have been a difficult conversation to have, Velumani's wife saw the intensity in her husband's self-belief. She then took the major step to support him: she resigned from her bank job and joined her husband to help him achieve his dream. With ₹1 lakh from his provident fund, Velumani, at the age of 37, opened the first Thyrocare shop. It was in Byculla, a middle-class neighbourhood in South Mumbai, near the Tata Memorial Hospital, a prominent cancer institute. Velumani started out with a franchise model, where samples would be collected across the country and sent back to the central laboratory in Mumbai. It was met with so much demand that Thyrocare expanded from testing for thyroid disorders to providing preventive medical check-ups and other diagnostic blood tests. Today, Velumani is the owner of the world's largest thyroid testing company [5].

So what prompted Velumani to take such a risky step, quitting his job and spending a large chunk of his provident fund, not knowing whether he would fail or succeed? Velumani had the conviction that his idea would be helpful to the world. He didn't shrink from fear of failure nor follow the naysayers and critics. Because he valued his idea and believed it would be worthwhile, he was able to move forward undaunted. This quality of Velumani's is something that many high achievers have in common: they are able to withstand and tolerate any form of setback simply on their belief that they can reach their goals.

Velumani's self-esteem enabled him to trust his own abilities and have faith in his vision. In other words, his healthy self-esteem was the foundation for his other personality strengths that enabled him to succeed. It was the breeding ground for his persistence and optimism. Most importantly, he believed that his hard work would enable him to overcome challenges and succeed. Knowing this, he was able to work long hours and push through countless struggles, risks and uncertainties.

Many studies and real-life examples have shown that developing strong and positive self-esteem is one of the keys to success. Experts have found that having an adequate sense of self forms an internal ecosystem for hope and persistence to thrive. This creates a positive growth cycle [6].

## TAPPING INTO INNER STRENGTH

Our self-esteem is determined by many factors identified by psychologists, including how well we view our own performance and appearance, and how satisfied we are with our relationships with other people.

Not only that, but our self-esteem does not stay at a constant level all the time. It keeps fluctuating, often day to day and even hour to hour [7]. When we succeed at an important task or do something useful, while feeling accepted and valued by others, this cultivates high self-esteem. And the contrary also happens: when we fail, do something harmful or feel that we are being marginalized, we are upset and crippled with self-doubt, and our self-esteem takes a hit. This yo-yo effect happens more frequently when we face complex challenges and competition in work, relationships and social media. It is, therefore, a thought process that can be changed. It is the force of our nature that can create a better life.

A person with a healthy self-esteem has positive mentality, inspiration and passion for creativity, productivity and, therefore, success. This sense of self helps us to achieve more in a joyful way. We can appreciate others' good fortune without getting into comparisons with others.

There is a woman in India who is a brilliant artiste. In fact, she can be considered a heroic personality. Her life was a dream as an accomplished Bharatanatyam dancer. But in all heroic tales, tragedy struck. 'I was travelling from Trichy by bus when, we met with a major accident that left me with a fracture and some cuts—I was probably the least injured. However, because of the heavy influx of patients, I was attended to by a couple of interns who forgot to attend to the cut on my right ankle and went ahead to wrap it up. This resulted in my foot getting gangrene and because of the fear of it spreading throughout my body, my parents had to take the difficult decision of amputating my right foot. I was shattered because it was only then that I realized just how passionate I felt about dancing' [8].

Sudha Chandran's passion had been crushed by the accident. One would imagine that her dream was crushed too, that she would just give in and forget about her first love: dance. But no, she didn't fall apart. With determination and willpower, she decided she would try to get back some remnant of her old life. She had heard about the Jaipur foot, an artificial limb, a rubber-based prosthesis for people with below-knee amputations. Chandran decided to get the prosthetic leg. She didn't hesitate to think about what people would say, or if this fake leg would be of help or a hindrance. She was resolute in her plan. The Jaipur foot was fitted perfectly to her limb. When she was able to stand, with painstaking effort she began to learn how to walk again. It took her four months to even be able to walk straight and three years of physiotherapy to feel normal again. Her self-belief was unbounded, she didn't let anyone affect her determination.

'I remember people would come home and say things like, "it's so sad your dreams can't come true" or "we wish you could dance" that's when I decided to re-learn what I had known my entire life—to dance.'

Chandran is living proof that anyone can reach their goal no matter how dire the circumstances. She had a healthy sense of self-value and she persisted. She could have lost confidence in her ability to dance. She could have compared herself to others and viewed herself as a disabled person. But she did none of that, she simply focused on her goal: to dance again. Her driving force was rooted in her self-confidence and her innate sense of self-esteem. Her motivations towards achievement stemmed from setting realistic goals.

'Finally one day, I went to my dad and told him that I was ready to perform again ... and he was shocked!'

The performance was at the St Xavier's College in Mumbai. The media headlines, 'Looses a Foot, Walks a Mile', created a buzz of interest. Her performance was considered a heroic achievement. Despite being nervous before going on stage, Chandran didn't back down nor did she display any signs of weakness.

'Believe it or not, the show ended, I performed the Varanyam with ease and received a standing ovation. When I was home, my dad came up to me and touched my feet saying that I'm touching the feet of the Goddess Sarasvati because you have done the impossible.'

That was a heartfelt moment for Chandran, she made it, achieved her dream. After all the pain, struggle and hours of practice, she was able to deliver a memorable performance; she received accolades and respect from the media. She was also offered a role to act in a film about her life.

Deep within herself, Chandran had created a positive mindset to use as a tool to achieve her goals. Her sheer willpower carried her to new heights of success, but it was self-esteem and persistence that gave her the initial spark to do it. She didn't dim her inner light nor downplay her strengths. Her talent was her pride and she knew she still had it in her to perform before an audience of thousands. Sudha Chandran has become one of the most beloved celebrities in India.

When Chandran was nervous before going up on stage, she recalled that her grandmother had told her to have faith in God who was always with her. 'What my grandmother said was true—God was with me. Even if I didn't see it then, he was with me all along and that's the irony of life—that an accident so fatal, can still be a blessing in disguise.'

Indeed a blessing in disguise that helped Chandran to discover her limitless inner strength.

## THE FUTILITY OF ATTACHMENT

In Buddhist and other Eastern thinking, there is a term known as grasping, which refers to clinging to a desire or a wish with mindless desperation. It is psychologically attaching to this wish with an inflexible grip. It is like clutching to the string of a kite that is not meant to stay in one position. This clinging stems from a desire to control. When we engage in this grasping impulse, self-esteem can be low or high. But this thinking process is unhealthy and unpleasant.

These messages from the East can serve us very powerfully in inviting us to take an approach to life that is less burdensome and more liberating. Imagine if we could approach our duties with a bit less intense grasping and more focused but relaxed action. Imagine a perspective in which you feel integrated with your external responsibilities and challenges. The idea of the 'self' need not be the 'be all' and 'end all' of life.

This perspective is observed in what Lord Krishna said to Arjuna in the ancient text of the Bhagavad Gita:

> Work for work's sake, not for yourself. Act but do not be attached to your actions. You have a right to perform your prescribed duties, but in one sense you are not entitled to the fruits of your actions. Work done with anxiety about results is far inferior to work done without such anxiety, in the calm of self-surrender. They who work selfishly for results are miserable.

The bottom line is to pursue your goals with equanimity, setting aside the fruits of your labour, that is, to be goal focused rather than reward focused. It is about being in the present moment and focusing on the job at hand. Eastern wisdom suggests that the right outcome will come at the right time in the right way. Clinging to a fantasy of a successful outcome and being impatient about it can lead to disappointment and cracks in one's self-esteem.

The great question is what we will do in the face of obstacles, frustrations and failure. Here, self-esteem and persistence (with some degree of non-attachment) can make all the difference. Setbacks will happen. They can be a learning experience which can enhance our capabilities going forward. On the other hand, in the absence of self-esteem, we become fragile and susceptible to judgements of others. As a result, we face greater risk of giving up.

The healthier our self-esteem, the more motivated we tend to be, not only professionally but also emotionally, spiritually, creatively and intellectually. We become more open and honest and feel that our thoughts and feelings have value. We are also willing to change, to overcome flaws. And we want to share ourselves with the world without hesitation. But when our self-esteem takes a beating, we become more hesitant. We withdraw, hide our light and withhold our best.

## **RESPECTING SENIORS**

In 2018, a digital consultant's tweet resulted in an uproar when it went viral on social media. She commented angrily: 'I absolutely despise how Indian companies and founders, with no concept of life-work balance, shame employees for taking leaves and having a life outside work', she tweeted. She also tweeted about the many workaholic bosses who expected employees to follow in their footsteps. 'And of course, there are jerks who proudly claim that when they got married, they were at work THE VERY NEXT DAY. The day we stop having founders and bosses like this, we can perhaps *start* to talk about mental health at workplaces.' Many people related with the post and even shared some of their 'bad bosses' experience. This led to her mentioning that there was lack of respect for work-life balance by Indian bosses.

'Calls on weekends, guilting a person during and post leave, infinite power games. Shameful.' The post received over a 1,000 retweets and 2,000 likes [9].

It's commonly accepted that the work culture in India embraces a hierarchy system where the bosses are treated with a kind of reverence. Starting from the joint family system, many Indians follow the same pattern of respecting seniors in the workplace with a kind of ingratiating behaviour, especially if the employee is in a highly sought-after career path. This kind of workplace environment results in a division between the managers and their juniors.

Quite often, the juniors are not treated with respect. They are expected to be available after-work hours and even on weekends. In one particular company, the HR was aware of the situation but remained silent, afraid of the boss, the founder. One particular employee commented: 'I was suffering from anxiety attacks, not getting enough sleep and eating at odd hours. I had hypertension and was on medication. I finally quit but was not given a release letter. I was humiliated. It was hell.'

In traditional cultures, especially in Asia, we learn not to challenge our seniors. Our elders are supposed to be treated and addressed with respect. Seniors are considered more experienced and wiser in the ways of the world. They are considered our guides and teachers. In many countries, this is even expressed physically in traditions of bowing. We might assume they are nearly perfect.

However, this kind of conditioning can go too far if you lose perspective. Often times, although the experience is awkward, a senior may come to a conclusion that is well-intentioned but ultimately off base or unhelpful. Although they deserve all the respect in the world, seniors too make mistakes. Depending on your upbringing, it can actually be difficult to recognize when they judge you wrongly. These issues can colour our experiences at work. When a senior manager makes a critical comment, we start to believe it as the truth. This can undermine our sense of self.

We are conditioned not to speak openly out of respect for authority. And as we grow up, anyone in a senior position is placed on a pedestal. These traditions of respect may help build family and community cohesion, but when I look within, I feel they have a downside for self-esteem. One tends to cower before elevated individuals. And the worst part is that when a senior criticizes our work and tells us we are not good enough, we believe them.

In the 1980s, Col Abhinav Singh was the commanding officer of his battalion of 200 men. The colonel was a sturdy, tall man with a stern expression and a short temper. As an upright commanding officer, he expected his unit to be the best. He was very particular about discipline and punctuality. He had not been tardy one day in his life. Col Singh was a tough task master. He was hard on himself and harder on his unit, who he pushed to achieve the highest possible standard. He was well known among his peers, as well as the other battalions, for castigating the slightest mistake of his subordinates. Few wanted to be in his unit. They believed that no one could ever achieve his gold standard of perfection, no matter how hard they tried. The officers on the receiving end of his reprimands were reduced to tears. The Colonel was stingy with his praise, in fact, no one had heard him offer a kind word or appreciation. Many secretly sought an assignment transfer.

One Sunday, Col Singh's unit was playing their weekly game of basketball. Two lieutenants were assigned as referees. The players, which included Col Singh, were divided into teams. An audience of other army men looked on with interest. It was a hard-fought game, and yet many of the officers steered clear of the Colonel or played him lightly. The game grew increasingly physical, however. Two players tussled over the ball. The referee, Lt Vijay, blew his whistle calling a foul. The Colonel was at fault, everyone watched in stunned silence. Such a confrontation was almost unimaginable. The second referee blew his whistle to confer, suggesting they carry on. Lt Vijay stopped the game again with his whistle, repeating the same foul call. He wouldn't be intimidated. All looked on in disbelief. Lt Vijay stepped before the Colonel and declared defiantly, 'If you do that again, you will be disqualified from the game!'

The Colonel's face turned beetroot red, like he would explode. The referee didn't back down. They stared each other down motionless, both standing their ground. The Colonel gave him a hint of a nod and turned away. With a blow of the whistle from the second referee, the game continued. But the story spread like wildfire through the unit. The officers expected Lt Vijay to be admonished by the strict Colonel and go into a total panic. When they warned Lt Vijay, he seemed unconcerned and relaxed. 'I was following the rules of the game', he shrugged.

Everyone was on edge in the aftermath of the game. Later that evening, when the men met at the bar for a drink, Col Singh walked in. Lt Vijay was chatting and sharing a drink with his friends, who had warned him that confronting the Colonel was a mistake. Col Singh went up to him. The space cleared around the two men as the others looked on apprehensively. Lt Vijay braced for the harshest reprimands imaginable. A silence descended over the space, everyone waiting with bated breath. Col Singh patted Lt Vijay on his shoulder and said, 'Well done Vijay. That is what is expected of officers—doing the right thing even if it is hard. I wouldn't have expected any less.' Col Singh said this in his typical strict veneer and offered the bewildered officer a drink.

Everyone's jaw dropped. Lt Vijay was momentarily stunned but recovered quickly and thanked Col Singh. Never had the Colonel displayed such positive emotion, let alone praise. It came as a shock to many who thought the Colonel was heartless. Didn't he enjoy making others tremble in fear? The moment passed without incident, as if nothing had happened. But it would become a story to be retold innumerable times, a lesson in standing in your own integrity. During the game there was no hierarchy. Col Singh was a player, not a senior officer. He knew the rules. And Lt Vijay knew his job, his role as a referee, and the Colonel admired this in the young man.

In this case, the self-esteem in question was that of the Colonel. As a youth, he looked up to his father who was also an army man, his disciplined approach spilled over into other areas of his life. He was hard on himself and harder on his son.

Maj. Gen. Neeraj Bali, a retired army officer, says, 'all bullies and autocrats cower when they are bullied right back. This is not to recommend shouting matches but occasionally standing up to him and giving him a glimpse of the steel within is helpful'.

Currently a Delhi-based leadership consultant, sharing strategies from his army life in advising executives on how to run their businesses effectively, Maj. Gen. Bali also added that, at core, every boss and leader is an amalgam of his 'nature and nurture'. Indeed, bosses, like the rest of us, are shaped by those around us, and part of this is imperfect parenting. The mistakes our parents made with us can lead us to demean others if we are not careful. If an employer lets his power go to his head, his focus and leadership ability can spiral downward [10].

## CULTURAL CONNECTIONS

Peter Nixon is a dialogue expert based in Hong Kong. In his many experiences, he has observed differences in Asian and American cultures in how they manage and communicate in organizations. Peter's tagline, 'The Solution Is in the Dialogue', is motivated by how misunderstandings can occur because of how different cultures communicate.

In his consultancy, he noticed that some Indian leaders have risen to their positions by 'climbing on shoulders of peers'. And they have grown up in an environment where the parents have unbelievably high expectations. He explained that in a 360-degree performance appraisal conducted by investment banks, Americans tend to rate themselves 5 out of 5, while Asians tend to rate themselves a 2 out of 5. This reluctance to boast is well known in Asian culture. Humility is fundamental. Thus, Asians tend to rate themselves at a level below their real performance [11].

Research shows that in certain cultures, people's self-esteem is derived through values of self-reliance, independence and assertiveness. This cultural influence is usually seen in Western countries such as the UK, certain parts of Europe, and some countries in South America. However, in the Middle Eastern, African and Asian countries, the emphasis is more on following traditional values, self-sacrifice, helping others and a sense of interconnectedness with others within a group. This cultural interaction is from where self-esteem is derived [12].

Social psychologists, Dr Vivian Vignoles and Dr Maja Becker, collaborated with a global team of researchers to understand what influences self-esteem. Dr Vignoles notes, 'Popular psychology and self-help books often seem to imply that people can build self-esteem on their own. These findings should remind us that no-one is an island. Building self-esteem is mostly a collaborative enterprise' [13].

## SELF-ESTEEM MOVEMENT

There was a self-esteem craze that took over America in the 1980s. The obsession was that increasing people's self-esteem could reduce crime, teen pregnancy and a host of other social ills—even pollution. In 1969 when psychotherapist Nathaniel Branden published *The Psychology of Self-esteem*, boosting self-esteem was viewed as the ultimate solution for all personal and social ills: 'I cannot think of a single psychological problem ... from that is not traceable to the problem of low self-esteem' [14]. Branden's ideas caught on quickly and soon became standard practice in the American educational system.

In the 1980s, the movement was started by an eccentric Californian politician named John Vasconcellos. He set up a task force to promote high self-esteem. His belief was that in order to thrive, people need to be treated with unconditional positivity. Since then, the self-esteem movement has helped transform the way the American children are raised. Increasingly, children were habitually showered with praise, regardless of what they achieved [15].

Roy Baumeister, a USA-based social psychologist, has argued that this kind of 'artificially pumping up self-esteem' has contributed to a measurable rise in narcissism.

Studies on the self-esteem movement discovered that it wasn't beneficial to simply be told that you are fabulous or wonderful. Feelings of self-doubt and uncertainty are part of life. We cannot entirely shield our loved ones from these feelings. The only way to build self-worth is through our actions. We have to put ourselves in difficult situations so that we can learn how to survive. We must face our challenges head-on to overcome the fear of failure [16].

Failure cultivates wisdom and maturity. These and other findings in the work of psychologist and author of *Grit: The Power of Passion and Perseverance*, Angela Duckworth, indicate that struggling builds character. We need to fail and experience discomfort, and over time, establish for ourselves a track record of success. Once you've proven to yourself that you can perform in front of a crowd or run a marathon or ask a person out on a date, it's a lot easier to face the next big challenge [17].

## FAIL BUT PURSUE YOUR DREAMS

CA Manav Vigg is in his early 40s and a published author. A few years ago, his self-esteem hit rock bottom when his first and only start-up in audio-visual content creation collapsed. The company performed extremely well in the first year and crashed with as much velocity in the following. Vigg and his partners ended up with huge debts.

'The lessons were learnt, and we were ready to pick up the pieces and start again. But I realized that people had lost faith in us. The same people who thought we had done great, started to call our efforts a big blunder. There were continuous calls from our creditors, but we couldn't furbish our loans in time. It got to the stage where I was terrified every time my phone would ring. We had not taken any money from unscrupulous elements. But you may find it surprising that even some of the most polished corporate professionals can stoop down to expletive language when denied timely payment of amounts which are otherwise pittance for them.'

Vigg was not only struggling with this sudden downturn in his life but faced criticism from family and friends. 'My parents referred to my self-proclaimed courageous attempt as a mistake that I should never repeat. And, therefore, I could never gather the courage to try again.'

For a long time Vigg couldn't attempt anything. 'Failure can damage your life in worse ways than you can imagine. It severely affects your self-confidence. It's irony that in our country where we value the Bhagavad Geeta, in the event of one failure, we deny people the chance to fulfil their karma to try again.'

The family emotional support came with its own riders. Vigg was constantly reminded of his colossal disappointment. His relatives would invite him for lunch only to counsel him that he should never have left his job. 'I countered back, would they have told me the same thing if I was a success? I realized from their expressions that they were so narrow in their views and faith in others.'

When Vigg tried to pitch to the same investors, they would remind him of the previous investments and losses. 'The only thing that kept me going during those times was this phrase from Shakespeare, "This too shall pass!" I decided to work on my dream to write a novel. I set my mind to hone my skills in storytelling. I wrote my first novel—*Confused Bastards*—and received some good reviews. I regained my self-esteem slowly but surely. Even though the novel has not been a huge success, it has helped me a lot. I finally realized that I was on the right track and am continuing to pursue my dream.'

Today, when Vigg looks at storytellers or even entrepreneurs who have made huge names for themselves, he has discovered that their secret to success is because they persisted. They kept on trying and were focused on their goals and not the end results. 'Your self-esteem is inside you. It is how you perceive yourself and how much you believe you can achieve your goals. If you perceive yourself with high self-esteem, and keep persisting, then sooner or later people will also believe in you [18].

## AFFIRMATIONS MAY NOT BE THE ANSWER

Popular ideas tell us to counter negative thinking with simple general positive affirmations. But there is research to suggest this can make things worse. Saying 'I'm a positive being', 'I am compassionate with others and myself', 'My ideas and opinions are highly valuable to the world', repeatedly through the day, only exacerbates the feelings of inadequacy. According to scholars, the problem is that it highlights the fact that there is something that needs to be fixed and reminds the person of his or her flaws.

Research shows that there are different ways we talk to ourselves. One is declarative self-talk which is quite simply just commenting on a situation which could be positive or negative. Another way is to question the self-talk [19].

To highlight the effectiveness of this style of self-talk, four groups of people were asked to solve a word puzzle. Before they started on it, the researchers asked each group to write: 'Will I', 'I will', 'I' or 'Will' repeatedly, 20 times on a separate piece of paper. When the groups worked on the puzzle, the group that wrote 'Will I' was able to solve nearly twice as many word puzzles than the rest of the groups.

This shows that when we question, we are more likely to be successful in achieving our goals. By simply telling ourselves to do something is not as effective as asking ourselves. With questions, we are able to reflect on negative beliefs and address fears that we can resolve. This form of questioning enables us to review what is holding us back. The research shows that all it takes is to ask rather than tell.

If you are about to give a speech, but feeling nervous, someone may say: 'I am really bad at speaking, I have always failed at it.' Another might give a positive spin and say: 'I will present a motivating and valuable talk which will be appreciated by my audience.'

Both styles of self-talk are declarative sentences. And even though one is positive and other negative, they both create a kind of pressure that weighs on the mind. These statements create anxiety and a sense of self-doubt.

However, if one of these sentences was switched to a question, it would make a huge difference: 'Am I really that bad at speaking? Haven't I had some good responses? Will I be able to deliver a motivating speech again?' The possible answers could be: 'I do forget my points at times and tend to be technical which may bore my audience when I talk. However, in my last presentation, I made a point that people found interesting and I really had their attention. How could I expand on that?' 'The last presentation that I did went well. What did I do that worked and how could I do more of that?'

This powerful strategy works better than affirmations because it acknowledges your negative thoughts and feelings and reduces the need to fight them. One starts to become an ally to the subconscious mind and elicits its cooperation. The subconscious mind is fantastic at coming up with creative solutions.

## THE BOTTOM LINE

Very often we hear people say: 'To me you're wonderful!', 'You're actually awesome', 'Why don't you appreciate yourself more?', or even worse 'Hey you should be more confident'. Unfortunately, these phrases do not improve self-esteem. Instead, they make a person feel inadequate or even guilty or afraid of being true to themselves.

Constantly doubting ourselves drains our life of vitality. When you want to improve your self-esteem, there is no need to strain aggressively. There is no need to punish yourself more! Imagine instead a light-handed approach. A problem long in development takes time to heal. There is no overnight shortcut to improve self-esteem, but there are steps we can take to grow.

One of the biggest lessons is to not give up when there are no grounds to do so. Persistence can foster self-esteem and self-esteem can in turn increase persistence, creating a positive feedback loop. This is a time-tested insight. By steadily moving forward we are making a commitment to affirming and building our own inner strength. In this way, our efforts over time can be transformative, if we are patient. Having an accepting attitude in the face of rejection or failure enables us to pick ourselves up and start fresh.

Above all else, approach these strategies with self-compassion. According to Kristin Neff, we must realize that we are perfect as people but our lives are imperfect and that is the shared human experience [20].

## REFERENCES

1. YouTube. The space between self-esteem and self-compassion: Kristin Neff at TEDxCentennialParkWomen [video]. YouTube; 2013. Available from: www.youtube.com/watch?v=lvtZBUSplr4
2. Bollywood film producer. Personal communication. 2018–2019.
3. Crocker J, Brook AT, Yu N, Villacorta M. The pursuit of self-esteem: Contingencies of self-worth and self-regulation. J. Pers. 2006;74(6):1749–1772. Available from: https://onlinelibrary.wiley.com/doi/abs/10.1111/j.1467-6494.2006.00427.x
4. Peck SM. The road less travelled. London: Rider; 1978. p. 24.
5. Bizztor. How an Indian farmer's son made 3,300 crores from just 10k. Bizztor; 2016. Available from: https://bizztor.com/dr-arokiaswamy-velumani/#
6. Baumeister RF, Campbell JD, Krueger JI, Vohs, KD. Does high self-esteem cause better performance, interpersonal success, happiness, or healthier lifestyles? Psychol. Sci. Public Interest. 2003 May;4(1):1–44. Available from: https://doi.org/10.1111/1529-1006.01431
7. Winch G. Five ways to build lasting self-esteem. Ideas. Ted.Com; 2016. Available from: https://ideas.ted.com/5-ways-to-build-lasting-self-esteem/
8. The Times of India. Sudha Chandran's story about her accident will leave you inspired. Times of India Blog; 2016. Available from: https://timesofindia.indiatimes.com/blogs/everything-social/sudha-chandrans-story-about-her-accident-will-leave-you-inspired/
9. Trends Desk. This Twitter thread calls out Indian bosses' 'no concept of work-life balance'. The Indian Express;

2018 August 27. Available from: https://indianexpress.com/article/trending/trending-in-india/work-life-balance-bad-indian-bosses-twitter-5326252/
10. Bali N. Phone interview. Delhi; 2020 May 18.
11. Nixon P. Phone interview. Hong Kong; 2020 July 21.
12. Konrath S. Self-esteem, culturally defined. In Scull A, editor. Cultural sociology of mental illness: An A-to-Z guide. Thousand Oaks, CA: SAGE Publications; 2014.
13. Bealing J. Research reveals the cultural origins of self-esteem. Medicalxpress.Com; 2014. Available from: https://medicalxpress.com/news/2014-02-reveals-cultural-self-esteem.html
14. Branden N. The psychology of self-esteem: a new concept of man's psychological nature. New York, NY: Bantam Books; 1983. p. 12.
15. Storr W. 'It was quasi-religious': the great self-esteem con. The Guardian; 2018. Available from: https://www.theguardian.com/lifeandstyle/2017/jun/03/quasi-religious-great-self-esteem-con
16. Yarian D. Is self esteem a misguided approach? Guidetoself helpbooks.Com; n.d. Available from: http://guidetoself helpbooks.com/self-esteem/is-self-esteem-a-misguided-approach/
17. Duckworth A. Grit: the power of passion and perseverance. New York, NY: Scribner; 2018.
18. Vigg M. Email interview. Delhi; 2020 July 11.
19. Senay I, Albarracin D, Noguchi K. Motivating goal-directed behavior through introspective self-talk: the role of the interrogative form of simple future tense. Psychol. Sci. 2010;21:499–504. Available from: https://doi.org/10.1177/0956797610364751
20. Neff K. The space between self-esteem and self-compassion [video]. TED (USA); 2013.

# CHAPTER 2

# LOOK AT YOURSELF RESPECTFULLY

*Judging a person does not define who they are.
It defines who you are.*

—Wayne Dyer

## AM I PERFECT YET?

'I was once a freak', says Riya Chandiramani, a 25-year-old Hong Kong based artist. In one of her articles, she recounts her gut-wrenching story of struggling with the eating disorder, anorexia [1].

Riya shares the complex combination of factors that led to her spiralling into the abyss of anorexia. While in school, she experienced a painful inner struggle stemming from feelings of not being good enough, comparisons with others and not valuing herself as an individual. Riya grew up an only child in an environment where she put others ahead of herself. She was a people pleaser. Her mother had an illness and Riya got the message that her own hardships are not something to share or burden others with. Despite everything Riya was going through in school and at home, she was a kind daughter and able student.

Her grades were great and outwardly she appeared balanced and happy. After she completed school, she wasn't quite sure what she wanted to study. To please others, she went along with whatever was suggested. She applied to the University of Pennsylvania and was accepted.

But her life changed after she moved to the USA. Socially, Riya struggled. She felt awkward interacting with boys and uncomfortable in the new world of American college life

She felt she had to step up to belong, to fit in among her peers. After a few months, she moulded herself to be one of them, at least outwardly. Internally, however, she hadn't changed much. She still felt alien, unsure and troubled by her inability to feel good about herself. She went about her routine, hoping she would eventually feel whole. In her second year, Riya was sexually assaulted. Feeling powerless to do anything about it, she said nothing. She was unable to confront the searing reality that she had been violated by another person. Like many victims, she instead blamed herself.

'I think that was the trigger, that's when I spiralled', Riya reflected.

As is commonly the case, she felt as though starving herself was a form of self-discipline or even virtue. It was done not out of some misguided desire to *look* perfect, so much as to *feel* a certain way. Underneath, it was somehow about punishment and reward. It was about feeling *in control*. She would work hard, exercise and when she stood on the scale, she could see the pay-off. Paradoxically, having an eating disorder can create a sense of purpose, or worthiness, because the sufferer can observe the visible 'results' of their hard work. This went on for months, and Riya went into depression. She saw the University counsellor, but they never identified the root cause of her problem. A few months later, when she returned to Hong Kong for Christmas, she revealed to her family her despair. In her family, mental health issues were not spoken of openly. At first, her parents were perplexed, and it was assumed that whatever she was experiencing would all fade away.

Feeling deflated, Riya dropped the matter. 'I was safe in this phase of having this power over my body', Riya explained.

But her body system was functioning erratically, her menstrual cycle stopped. 'I grew severely ill. All that time I didn't realize I had an eating disorder. I came to realize much later that I had a problem when my mental strength declined. My motivation to live fell to the wayside. People started to notice me for different reasons. I felt like a freak, my hipbones jutted out, my stomach was concave and my legs looked like they might snap in two.'

In her final year of University, things got worse. Riya noticed that her gums started receding due to malnutrition. She would need to see a dentist for surgery. While she was prepped, the nurse checked her pulse and then looked at her in shock, 'Are you alive?'

'I realized something was seriously wrong', Riya recalled. She was at rock bottom and her mind was fuzzy. She couldn't stop what she was doing to herself. But a small voice within told her the truth: deep down, she knew she couldn't continue to live this way. Riya broke down and called her parents. They flew to Philadelphia to see her. 'They were anxious and worried about me. They consulted with doctors, and more tests were done. The EKG showed that I was almost going to have a heart attack. My weight was of my 12-year-old self, and I was 21. Everyone was trying to help, but I was not able to accept their help. The physicians recommended that I receive residential treatment.'

Riya became so exhausted she essentially lost her capacity to decide what to do. 'I might have felt in control, but I ultimately lived in utmost fear. I was tangled in an abusive relationship with this powerful demon living within me', she added.

At the treatment centre, Riya slowly recovered, 'The counsellors focused on core beliefs, not body image. There were others like me, people from different backgrounds, but we had commonalities in the way we viewed ourselves and our childhood life map.' Contrary to popular belief, Riya did not 'get' anorexia from wanting to look like a super-skinny model. She subconsciously wanted to gradually disappear and ultimately vanish entirely. Asking 'why' she developed anorexia would be like asking an alcoholic 'why' they drink in the sense that the reasons are complicated, multiple and rooted in many more biological and environmental factors, often from childhood.

Riya's pre-teen years were a troubled time for her self-esteem. She would repeatedly compare herself with her best friend and felt inferior. She didn't think she was pretty. At home, there were times when her mother, a small-framed woman, said she wanted to lose weight. Riya was also compared to other children who seemed to have a better university or career path.

Riya was impacted by those words. 'Many details and conditioning started to hurt, and they become ingrained, they leave a scar. It's so important for parents to understand that children are affected by what they hear. I later realized as I got older that the love and acceptance must come from within me.'

Riya began the difficult journey of recovery. As is not uncommon, even her forward progress was at times marked by unhelpful perfectionism. There were times she was concerned she wasn't recovering 'correctly'. Thoughts of shame and guilt from her sexual assault at times would consume her. But with courage, patience and therapy, she would forge ahead.

'I have always heard the saying, "How can you expect anyone to love you if you don't love yourself?" and thought it was stupid. I would then wonder, "What does loving yourself even mean?" I thought self-love would be equated with narcissism, egotism and self-indulgent behaviour.'

Due to the trauma of her victimization, Riya's journey to greater self-esteem was particularly difficult. But she has learned to understand herself better.

She still struggles sometimes, but she knows how to handle those dark feelings. Once she learned to stop seeking external validation, life became happier and easier—she reports that her final year at university was her best. 'I was finding myself, not caring about what others think, considering my own needs and following my passions' [2].

One would think that eating disorders stem from poor body image issues, but no, it is not so. It goes far deeper than that. The exact causes of eating disorders are multi-fold: many factors contribute to the condition, including a person's personality, mental health, genetic and biological factors, and social environment. The reasons are different for each person. In terms of psychological reasons, they include low self-esteem, need to be perfect, social pressure and so on.

According to global statistics, about 20 per cent of teenagers will experience depression before they reach adulthood. One in six people, aged 10–19 years, is suffering from depression. The consequences of not addressing adolescent mental health conditions extend to adulthood, impairing both physical and mental health and limiting opportunities to lead fulfilling lives as adults [3].

Teenage girls that have a negative view of themselves are four times more likely to take part in activities with boys that they end up regretting later. The top wish among all teenage girls is for their parents to communicate better, more frequently and more openly with them [4].

We live in a culture that is obsessed with everything: beauty, popularity and likes. This results in judgement, criticism, seeking an unattainable ideal. Fat is 'bad', dark is 'ugly' and thin is 'weak'. These too much, too little, not good enough judgements impact our sense of self-worth. The adage 'beauty is skin deep' seems almost passé.

## BODY IMAGE MATTERS

Body shaming is defined as 'the action or practice of humiliating someone by making mocking or critical comments about their body shape or size'. Almost every individual has experienced body shaming irrespective of their gender, ethnicity, religion, caste or race. The way we feel is constantly influenced by our external surroundings. We are exposed to television commercials, social media and all manner of technology-related updates. These non-stop inputs and feeds, whatever the form, affect the way we feel about our identity, relationships, career, social status and increasingly our bodies.

Taking pictures has become much easier and as a result people post millions of selfies on social media sites daily. Just about everyone with a smartphone has an album full of personal photos. Snapping a selfie may seem like a nice way to capture a memory, but it actually has a major impact on self-esteem. When you take a selfie, you can't help but to evaluate your appearance and compare to others. Unlike prior eras when you had to wait for a photo to be printed, now you instantly view the result. You scrutinize your posture, your hair, your clothing, your makeup—anything that may look even slightly off the standard set by trending fashions. Your flaws are all too clear. With imaging software at our fingertips, any picture can be altered and refined for online sharing. As your inner critic takes centre stage, selfies become the modern-day axe, chopping down our inner joy. The more time we spend on social media, the more demanding standards become and the more susceptible we become to trolls who heartlessly magnify imperfections out of all proportions.

Our self-esteem topples over and gets crushed by hundreds of comments and impressions. We add our own masala of self-loathing to the mix. We are easily rocked from our mantle of inner balance by some stranger from half-way around the world. A few words can disrupt our day, get us into an irritable mood. This is if the self-esteem is vulnerable.

We hope that our self-esteem provides us with equanimity and resilience in the face of criticism. Ideally, a strong sense of identity enables us to remain firm against senseless negativity. But in today's technological world, our mind's protection is whittled away.

In a split second, people judge each other based on how we present ourselves. In a culture that tends to emphasize the superficial, a person's physical appearance has a powerful impact. It's usually not intentional but just part of our mental hardwiring. Harsh judgement is meted out towards those who don't conform to certain physical standards.

Vidya Balan, a popular Hindi film actress, faced heartless personal attacks involving her body shape that severely affected her self-esteem. In 2019, she courageously shared how painful this was in a video that went viral. She shared how jokes that targeted her appearance left a lasting impact on her life [5].

In an interview with the *Hindustan Times*, Vidya confessed, '[There was] a part of my life, I was in a battle with my body. I was angry with it, hated it and I wanted it to change, because I thought if my body changed, then I would be acceptable to everyone. I would be worthy of love. But even at my thinnest, when I managed to lose a lot of weight [it happened a few times], I realized that I wasn't fully acceptable to everyone. So really there's no point in trying to change yourself to suit others' needs and ideals' [6].

She has endured self-esteem difficulties despite her beauty, talent and successful career. It might be surprising that she felt that she wasn't good enough, but the criticism left her in self-doubt. In a candid chat with the Huffington Post, she suggested, 'stop fighting your body. It's the only place you have to live. This is what I've learned through the years. I fought and hated my body for a long, long time. A lot of young girls might have these body issues but you've to work towards loving and accepting yourself.'

Besides Vidya Balan, other celebrities have also faced body shaming. It has become common practice for many people to make nasty comments without realizing how damaging it can be. Public figures face a never-ending stream of judgement and criticism from both anonymous internet trolls and people in the real world.

Media has played a significant role in promoting the culture of body shaming. The film industry has helped establish unachievable beauty standards that seem to affect the thinking of many. Cosmetics advertisements stigmatize darker skin tones by preaching the beauty of fairer skin, while food and diet advertisements promulgate unachievable standards of weight loss and thinness.

With the increasing use of social media, body shaming has become a toxic pastime. From the safety of their home computer, mindless internet users attack others and post negative comments. Perhaps they can't imagine how their comment might harm someone. But every detrimental comment adds up.

Sarah Gervais, PhD, of *Psychology Today* points out how Instagram is trying to address these problems by making eating disorder specific keywords and hashtags unsearchable. But limiting the online experience to 'positive or selective' content might not help. It's a catch-22, the more information and attention given to the body, the higher the risk of becoming obsessed with the impossible beauty ideals. Gervais advises users to limit the amount of time one spends viewing social media. It is a matter of limits and using it wisely [7].

## FASHION FACTORS

What we wear impacts how we feel about ourselves. And that, in turn, influences our work. Our confidence, creativity and ability to collaborate is affected. Studies have provided evidence for the idea that the way people present themselves makes a difference in their self-esteem. And added to that is the comparing with others. Self-concept and self-esteem are also heavily influenced by the process of social comparison [8].

The media does play a big role in a person's body image and how one feels about oneself. It happens consciously and unconsciously, the comparisons are made of 'perfect' images of people in magazines, commercials, films and social media. It exists in every culture.

Clothing is a significant part of this sense of self-worth. The clothes we wear daily reflect the way we want others to perceive us and how we see ourselves. For fashion aficionados, clothing style is a way to express one's unique identity. All of this can affect our mental state in positive and negative ways.

Leon Festinger, a social psychologist from the 1950s, described an emotional state called cognitive dissonance, which means feeling discomfort when modes of thought contradict each other. He pointed out that when personal beliefs and actions do not align, one or the other will change so as to remove the source of discomfort. Usually, this leads to justifying the actions rather than changing the behaviour [9].

Sometimes we want to imitate someone else's style of dress because they look fabulous in it; however, we may find that the same clothes don't look that great on us. This may come as a shock. We might decide to never wear that outfit again.

Journalist Camay Abraham has a specialization in applied psychology in fashion. She says that we may face cognitive dissonance in the way we dress. This is a phenomenon where we feel certain clothes don't align with our style, beliefs or values. The resulting tension causes us unease. To reduce the discomfort, we either change into the clothes we are comfortable in so that they align with our beliefs again or we convince ourselves that the clothes are actually what we want to wear.

The point is this: should one choose what to wear based on how one feels or should one wear clothes to change how one feels?

Camay Abraham suggests that dressing to change how you feel is ideal. It inspires one towards a confident frame of mind, which also influences how others perceive you in a positive way.

The way we dress affects our mental well-being. Our tastes in fashion are indicators of our style and personality; it is a form of self-expression. This in turn affects how others treat us. Abraham says that if we wear the latest fashions, people's perceptions of us may be more accepting, as we are following the society's trends [10].

Therefore, how we dress is also an indicator of how we wish to be treated and accepted by our social groups. Clothes are an outer expression of how we feel and how we want others to perceive us.

## CORPORATE CLOTHING AFFECTS BUSINESS

Depending on the corporate culture, appearing poorly dressed, untidy and no make-up have been shown to result in worse self-esteem than if one appears well dressed, nicely groomed and nicely made up. The work environment is changing and, therefore, the office dress codes are also evolving. Does the experience of getting dressed every morning become troublesome or easy?

It depends on the profession. Some companies prefer uniform dress code and others require casual or formal attire.

No doubt, a uniform simplifies the process of getting ready every morning. Some companies prefer that their staff wear a standardized outfit. In a competitive environment, a well-thought professional work attire reinforces the company brand. Those in the hospitality or health and fitness industry would encourage that their employees where uniforms that have the corporate logo. This in turn creates a psychological effect and employees feel that they are the face of the business. They then behave in a more appropriate manner and feel a sense of pride in their work. In addition, when people wear the same type of clothing, there is a sense of camaraderie and a greater sense of team support.

Some companies have a relaxed dress code. This can be an advantage too. The overall attire and look can actually give a lasting impression of being smart and respected. Image makes a huge difference in how people perceive you. If you choose a right type of style, anyone can feel your confidence and will then look up to you. These feelings then manifest into a higher self-esteem [11].

In other office cultures, like finance and banking industries, there is a requirement of formal attire. The way one dresses in the workplace affects how they perceive themselves and how they are perceived by others. People who are in formal attire have an attitude that they can achieve greater success and power. They feel more confident about their abilities. Many studies have shown that how we dress and how we behave are definitely correlated [12].

When George went for an interview for a banking job, he wore a bright-coloured suit and fashionable shoes. In the first instance, he was rejected. It wasn't for reasons of bias or discrimination that George failed his interview, but common sense. He didn't check the culture of attires in different industries.

Fashion is a huge multi-crore industry telling us that we can look great and feel great too. How we value ourselves can be lousy one minute, but an outfit that accentuates our look can make us feel great in the next.

Fashion psychology is defined as the study of how colour, fashion and body shape impact human behaviour. Every morning we decide what to wear, and based on how we feel, or want to feel, that day, we put together an outfit. Clothes are linked to our identity, our desire to be unique. There is a quest for originality more than loyalty to a brand.

Western fashion trends have influenced the rest of the world, but this is evolving. People are open to fashion from other countries, and fusion fashion concepts have blended different cultural sensibilities. For example, new styles are mindful of religions in which individuals cover themselves but are still fashionable underneath.

A famous study showed how wearing a white coat impacts our perception of ourselves. The study found that when individuals were told that the garment was a lab coat, they performed tasks better, with greater focus and clarity, while for those who were told that it was a simple painter's coat, there was no improvement in their performance. This perception of identity based on what we wear, in psychology lingo, is called 'enclothed cognition'. It shows that one piece of clothing can have a monumental effect on self-perception [13].

If a man wears a suit, is he perceived differently than if he wears jeans and a basic tee? Yes. There is a difference in perception according to psychologists. As you might imagine, the suit conveys the sense that the man is educated, intelligent and paid well.

From research and experience, image does carry a great impact, and what one wears does make an impression in the minds of others and affects a person's self-perception. Clothes and fashion influence how we present ourselves at work and social environments. So, if we are wearing attire that gets that appreciative vibe, it raises our self-esteem.

## DERIVING SELF-WORTH FROM EXTERNAL FACTORS

Mel Schwartz, a psychotherapist and marriage counsellor, says that self-esteem tends to be misunderstood. 'The first half of the expression, *self*, would seem to indicate that *esteem*, the second half of the expression, is derived from one's self. Yet if we look closer, we find that most people seek a sense of worthiness from that which lies outside' [14].

The sense of worthiness might come from getting good marks in school or university, or even receiving a promotion. 'For most individuals, praise or acknowledgment provides a temporary increase in esteem. Countless advertisements for products induce people to seek quick fixes. Yet none of these actually contribute one iota to self-esteem.'

Ironically, they may even get in the way. When self-esteem is sought from external sources, we are never sure what our feelings will be in the next moment. According to Schwartz, what we call self-esteem is, in fact, other esteem. Wishing to be liked by someone else leads to inadequacies in oneself, in distrusting our own strengths.

Those who have a low sense of self-worth tend to believe that they will not be able to do better anywhere else, so they cling desperately to what they have, even if it is a failed relationship or a dead-end job. This sense of insecurity avoids taking risks and discovering one's true potential. Low self-esteemers experience a sense of desperation and a need to constantly self-validate.

We should never judge ourselves based upon how we think others see us. When we are looking for approval from others, we are actually denying our own self, we are not giving our self a chance to do what we want to do. We do what we expect will get us the most compliments or the praise. Doing what you value, what you feel intrinsically is more important. If you live your life from a false self, denying your unique qualities, you end up later with: 'I didn't want to do this, but I did because it would make so-and-so impressed.' This is an unhealthy and soul-defeating exercise. The key to trusting ourselves and developing our own self-esteem is found by accepting our own fears and vulnerabilities. There is no shame in being imperfect, says Schwartz.

Being comfortable in one's own skin is what makes anyone look good. Author of the *100 Simple Secret* series, David Niven, a noted psychologist and social scientist, says that many of our feelings of satisfaction or dissatisfaction have their roots in how we compare ourselves to others. When we compare ourselves to others who have more, we feel a deep lack. When we compare to those who have less, we feel grateful. Our feelings change merely based on who we compare ourselves with.

When we are upset with ourselves because someone else is a better cook or employee or living the perfect life, we belittle who we are as unique individuals. We get so wrapped up in envy that we are frozen in a state that we cannot see our own good qualities.

Self-esteem rises to a new level of importance in our plugged-in hypercritical world. There is so much going on around us from the moment we wake up to the moment we close our eyes that thoughts and feelings are left unchecked. We must be even more alert of how everything around us affects how we feel.

## BEATING BULLIES

Brijesh P. is a 34-year-old Indian man from a traditional and conservative family. He was born in India, but his parents migrated to Hong Kong when he was just a toddler. As a child growing up in an international school, he was constantly bullied. Being a chubby, plump boy, he was the butt of many jokes. 'I was laughed at because I was so fat. I had man boobs. The local kids chose other parts of my body to make fun of. Some of the kids would call me Pinocchio because of the size of my nose. My own friends would tease me about my body size. I desperately wanted to fit into the school, and I thought if I was accepted by a few friends, the bullying would stop. Their words hurt, but I just laughed along with them.'

Brijesh didn't tell his parents, nor did he confide in his older sister. Brijesh didn't want to come across as weak. He didn't want to bother anyone. Every morning, he would dread going to school and would find some excuse to stay home. When that didn't work, he would find ways to skip classes. His grades were terrible, and he lived in constant fear of being ridiculed and harassed.

## Chapter 2: Look at Yourself Respectfully

'If you are bullied, you remember it forever. It's something that sticks to you. School life was torment. When I saw the bullies, my heart pounded fast; my brain would go blank. When the bully called out insults, the other kids would giggle at me, making me feel alone and awkward. No one stood by me and told the bully to back off', said Brijesh.

Bullying is particularly painful to a young mind navigating social pressures. The bullies were from all different backgrounds and cultures, including some Indians too. As Brijesh was in his pre-teen years, he became very self-conscious about the way he looked. Besides his low grades, he was bad at sports as well. He took a deep hit to his self-esteem. He kept up an outward semblance of being fine, but internally he was deeply pained.

How does a bully pick his victim? They sniff them out, guessed Brijesh, just like how dogs can sniff out fear. 'I figured that because I came across with low confidence and nervous, these kids could sense my weaknesses and they would attack. I wanted to fight back, but I did not know how, and nobody really helped me. I felt I would lose the few friends I had, so I sucked it up.'

This went on for seven years. There was never a break, a moment to catch his breath, never a moment where Brijesh could feel relaxed. The insults increasingly bore down on his spirit.

It has been presumed that children who bully are the kind who are aggressive with self-esteem issues and are from troubled homes and families. However, says Dorothy Espelage, a professor of education, that picture is now changing. There is another more destructive kind of bullying. Children who fall into this category are friendly, likeable by teachers and are not crude, they are able to turn on and off their bullying to suit their needs.

'Socially dominant bullies want to be the leader of the crowd', says Espelage. 'And the way that they do that is to push kids down the hierarchy.'

Victims of bullying tend to have high levels of insecurity, depression, anxiety and low self-esteem, but it's nearly impossible to tell if these feelings are the cause or the effect of bullying. The irony is that kids who bully often experience the same emotions and some of the kids who are bullied also bully others. Not surprisingly, these aggressor victims have the highest rates of depression and anxiety [15].

In his teen years, Brijesh managed to endure this deprecating onslaught by making changes in his own life. 'I didn't know how to retaliate, but as I grew older, I began to realize a few things about myself. I did know I was going to find a way to stand up to those bullies. I am resilient when I set my mind to something. And I didn't want to fake it anymore. I didn't want to fit in or prove I was cool like the others. I became stronger as I grew up. I chose to rebel against the norm. I drew strength by being true to myself. I am a bit quirky and different, and I realized that I am okay with that. The bullies eventually sensed my rebellious attitude and would back off.'

At the age of 16, Brijesh decided that he wanted to lose the flab and get fit. He had a plan to lose weight. He would go for a run few hours every day. It was tough initially, but he pushed through. While most of his loved ones supported him, some didn't. His uncle laughed at him and mocked, 'Why are you trying so hard? You'll never be thin.' It felt like the bully was at home too!

Brijesh didn't let his uncle's words sour his determination. Brijesh believes the running enhanced his self-esteem and sense of achievement as he lost the weight. He gained confidence through his own efforts. 'I realized that my self-worth was so important. If I don't respect my body and my mind, no one else will.' Brijesh studied a number of self-help books. He also stayed very socially active, volunteering regularly and joining a spiritual organization. He gained inner strength and was able to face the bullies. His fear lessened and ultimately disappeared. In fact, 'I felt sorry for them. They must have had their own

## Chapter 2: Look at Yourself Respectfully                                      43

issues or were bullied at home. I was stronger and gave off a confident vibe. I think that's what made a difference.'

Brijesh's final year in school was better, but his study habits were still poor. His 'A' level grade results were bad. He got three Ds, which would make it hard for him to get into a good university. His father told him to forget about university and start working in their family-owned business. He would have to start at the bottom as a dishwasher. Brijesh was shaken, 'It was a light bulb moment. My father's words were a sharp jolt of reality.' His sister urged him to beg their father to give him a chance.

Brijesh took her advice and implored for a chance to apply in the UK. His father finally relented and agreed on a condition that he got into a university and studied hard. It was difficult. Brijesh had to find a university that would accept him. Brijesh prayed and promised that if he got into university, he would work tenaciously to prove he was capable.

Being away from Hong Kong motivated Brijesh to change. And the 'dishwasher threat' lurked at the back of his mind as he received one rejection letter after another. He didn't give up. He, finally, was accepted into a business school. 'I became a serious student, sitting in the front row in all my classes, taking notes and staying on top of homework.'

During that time, Brijesh made great friends. 'I experienced one incident that brought back memories of school. A hulking Indian guy wanted to fight me. I didn't want to appear weak, so I agreed. Fear gripped me, as if I was back in the school yard. The fight was planned for the evening that day. I was shit scared, and I told my German friend who is a decade older. My friend said, don't worry, I will come with you. We will take on this guy together.' Brijesh was deeply touched by his response. If only he had friends like that in school, 'someone who would stand by me when the bullies attacked'. When Brijesh and his friend reached the designated place, the guy didn't turn up.

Brijesh immersed himself in student groups and his various classes. In the first semester, he performed so well that he ranked the highest in his class. It was a thrilling moment. His parents were proud of him. Brijesh knew he could achieve great heights. And the scars from his past faded in the background. After four years in university, he graduated and found a job in sales. Brijesh is a happy man and has a life that he built on his own terms. Whenever Brijesh notices a person being bullied, he makes sure to show support.

Brijesh's early experiences were painful. However, he chose to overcome his feelings of despair and develop a mindset that would lead to change [16].

## MINDSET MATTERS

People with a fixed mindset have a need to protect their ego and may get very defensive when someone suggests they made a mistake; in other words, they measure themselves by their failures. People with a growth mindset, on the other hand, often show perseverance and resilience in the face of errors—they become motivated to work harder. Carol Dweck's, a Stanford University psychologist, findings suggest that success is 90 per cent attitude.

Dweck popularized the idea of mindsets. She defines mindset as a simple idea that has a profound effect on a person's life. 'Mindset is the view that you accept for yourself, what determines the way you live your life, see the world and make decisions.' After decades of research into people's beliefs about themselves and their abilities, Dweck identified two fundamental mindsets that people have.

The first is a fixed mindset, which thinks that our abilities are innate or unchangeable. Our thoughts are rigid and conditioned. If we stick to a belief system, we are not able to look at an alternate point of view. When this mindset is predominant, failure can be unsettling because it makes us doubt ourselves from the root of who we are.

The other way of thinking is the growth mindset, which means we expect that we can improve our basic qualities and capabilities. In this mindset, failure is not so problematic, for it shows us how to change and learn from our mistakes. We accept that change is inevitable and in an ephemeral world, adapting to new ideologies and trends is necessary to stay in sync with the new generation. Resisting change affects our own mindsets [17].

Many people are afraid to change or push towards a goal because they feel that other people will not approve, or they may lose respect if they fail. It is true there are people who will judge or resent us for wanting to aspire to a goal. But that is a choice that one must make based on one's own mindset.

If you have a growth mindset, you are never too old to learn. John Basinger is a prime example of this. At 58, Basinger began memorizing Milton's epic poem *Paradise Lost*. Nine years and thousands of study hours later, he completed this process in 2001 and recalled from memory all 12 books of this 10,565-line poem over a 3-day period. Now 74, he continues to recite this work [18].

In the ideas advocated by Dweck, Basinger's feat shows that our potential for greatness is untapped, it is created by our mindset and how we think about ourselves. We are all born with certain skills, but our attitude towards improving them and ourselves ultimately determines our success in life. There are many heroic people who inspire and motivate others to overcome problems to achieve their full potential.

## WE LEARN FROM THE LIVES OF OTHERS

Malala Yousafzai offers another inspiring example of the growth mindset. Malala was only 10 years old when Taliban fighters took control of her region. Their strict beliefs dictated women could not go to the market and girls could not go to school. Malala was raised in Pakistan, and she was raised to stand up for what is right. So she fought for her right to be educated. And on 9 October 2012, she nearly lost her life for the cause: She was shot point-blank while riding the bus on her way home from school. Not only did she survive, but she has become an international symbol of peaceful protest and the youngest Nobel Peace Prize winner.

Struggle and even failure can be an ally in our development. We discover our limitations and grow from there, changing and adjusting to the twists and turns of life. We accept too what we cannot change and pursue other ways to achieve our goals. The growth mindset provides a pathway to greater happiness and success. And most importantly, to accept ourselves as we are. From there the seed of self-esteem will be nourished.

## BOTTOM LINE

The more we subject our minds to perfect images of others, the more we believe that we can change the way we look. Even if we are genetically a certain shape or size, and even if we are culturally distinct, we convince ourselves that we can transform ourselves to meet a certain ideal. There is so much pressure to live up to beauty and fitness standards that we are taught to compare ourselves to others, instead of embracing our own beauty. The sense of worthiness and the ability to connect emotionally to one's self and to others are often linked to a positive body image.

    The intolerance of body diversity is ultimately a sort of prejudice. Being thin, toned and muscular has become associated with being hard working, successful, popular, beautiful, strong and disciplined. For some reason, being fat is associated with being lazy, indulgent, weak and lacking in willpower. This form of prejudice is no less pernicious than the other forms.

This judgementalism makes daily life worse for those who do not fit the perfect ideal. Having a positive self-image involves understanding that healthy attractive bodies come in many shapes and sizes. If we base our happiness on how we look, what we wear, it can lead to frustration and undermine our pursuit of happiness.

Being healthy is more important than being perfect according to some arbitrary standard. We cannot change our body type: thin or plump, small or large, short or tall. But we can appreciate the uniqueness of who we are. Although our experiences of our own body sometimes include hardships, our body is the vehicle that carries us through life.

We need to take care of our bodies and appreciate what it is doing for us.

The truth about fashion is that what we wear reflects our thoughts and tastes. If we depart from our best vision of who we are, it may not benefit our wellness. Dressing exceptionally will increase our self-esteem to a great extent. Accordingly, follow your best sense of what is fashionable and socially sound. It can be a source of joy and even empowerment.

We all have our strengths. What is important is not how we compare to others but how we compare to where we were yesterday, last week or last year.

When we accept ourselves and others, we can move forward and develop in the areas that we care most deeply about. Really, that's all that matters.

## REFERENCES

1. Chandiramani R. 20 lessons I learned from anorexia. Medium; 2017 March 26. Available from: https://medium.com/@riyachandiramani/20-lessons-i-learned-from-anorexia-8f0f3c5ebf76

2. Chandiramani R. Email interview; 2020 May.
3. India Today. India is the most depressed country in the world. India Today; 2019 June 17. Available from: https://www.indiatoday.in/education-today/gk-current-affairs/story/india-is-the-most-depressed-country-in-the-world-mental-health-day-2018-1360096-2018-10-10
4. DoSomething.org. 11 facts about teens and self esteem. DoSomething.org; n.d. Available from: https://www.dosomething.org/us/facts/11-facts-about-teens-and-self-esteem#:~:text=Teen%20girls%20that%20have%20a
5. Chaubey P. Vidya Balan's video on body shaming gets lots of love from the internet. NDTV.Com; 2019 May 29. Available from: https://www.ndtv.com/entertainment/vidya-balans-video-on-body-shaming-gets-lots-of-love-from-the-internet-2044955
6. Vidya Balan breaks down while addressing body-shaming in heart-wrenching video, Twitter says 'take a bow'. Hindustan Times; 2019. Available from: https://www.hindustantimes.com/bollywood/vidya-balan-breaks-down-while-addressing-body-shaming-in-heart-wrenching-video-twitter-says-take-a-bow/story-DLucD3HG1IpY6vhOxXVN8M.html
7. Gervais S. Does Instagram promote positive body image? Psychology Today; 2013. Available from: https://www.psychologytoday.com/us/blog/power-and-prejudice/201301/does-instagram-promote-positive-body-image
8. Stangor C. The social self: the role of the social situation. In: Jhangiani R, Tarry H, editors. Principles of social psychology. 1st international edition. Victoria: BCcampus; 2014 September 26. Available from: https://opentextbc.ca/socialpsychology/chapter/the-social-self-the-role-of-the-social-situation/

9. Mcleod S. Cognitive dissonance. Simply Psychology; 2014. Available from: https://www.simplypsychology.org/cognitive-dissonance.html
10. Dittrich A. How fashion impacts our mental wellbeing. DW.COM; 2019. Available from: https://www.dw.com/en/how-fashion-impacts-our-mental-wellbeing/a-50562794#:~:text=In%20making%20this%20decision%2C%20fashion
11. Shoket A. How power dressing moved beyond the high heel. Thriveglobal.Com; 2018. Available from: https://thriveglobal.com/stories/power-dressing-beyond-high-heel-status-symbol-change-fashion-psychology
12. Shinn A, Swigart A, Gritters A, Schmailzl M. Dress codes in the workplace: effects on organizational culture—writing anthology. Central.Edu; 2011. Available from: https://www.central.edu/writing-anthology/2019/06/04/dress-codes-in-the-workplace-effects-on-organizational-culture/
13. Maldonado A. Clothes as therapy (enclothed cognition). The Psychology of Fashion; 2020. Available from: https://magazine.psykhefashion.com/features/fashion-psychology-enclothed-cognition
14. Schwartz M. Self esteem or other esteem? 2013 July 29. Available from: https://melschwartz.com/self-esteem-or-other-esteem-2/
15. Oakes K. Why children become bullies at school. BBC Future; 2019. https://www.bbc.com/future/article/20190913-why-some-children-become-merciless-bullies
16. Hong Kong resident. Face-to-face interview. 2020 August 2.
17. Careers in Psychology. Fixed mindset vs growth mindset: your success hinges on it. 2014. Available from: https://careersinpsychology.org/fixed-vs-growth-mindset-success/

18. Seamon JG, Punjabi PV, Busch EA. Memorising Milton's *Paradise Lost*: a study of a septuagenarian exceptional memoriser. Memory. 2010;18(5):498–503. Available from: https://doi.org/10.1080/09658211003781522

# CHAPTER 3

# IMPOSTER SYNDROME

*The fundamental cause of trouble in the world today is that the stupid are cocksure while the intelligent are full of doubt.*

—Bertrand Russell

## FEELINGS OF FAKERY

If you have read Michelle Obama's memoir, *Becoming*, you will have heard about imposter syndrome. The former first lady of the USA has experienced this feeling, which literally means a persistent internalized fear of being exposed as a fraud. Despite her many accomplishments, she still feared the book wouldn't sell and her tour would be a flop. Her book has sold over 11.7 million copies since then.

Many successful celebrities, leaders and entrepreneurs have described a feeling like they have fooled the world into thinking that they are capable, talented and worthy. They feel like frauds and believe they will be exposed at any moment. This is the definition of imposter syndrome. It is experienced by people at all levels and in all walks of life, although women and minorities suffer disproportionately.

In 1978, the term imposter phenomenon, the precursor idea to imposter syndrome, was coined by psychological researchers Pauline Clance and Suzanne Imes. Clance defined imposter phenomenon as 'an internal experience of intellectual phoniness that those who feel fraudulence and worthlessness have in spite of outstanding academic or professional accomplishment'. The researchers initially thought it was a kind of anxiety unique to women, but later realized it was far more prevalent. In the mid-1980s, Clance teamed up with Gail Matthews, now a professor of psychology at Dominican University of California, to conduct a survey on this feeling of fakery. They found that about 70 per cent of people from all walks of life—men and women—have felt like imposters for at least some part of their careers. That's when they knew they were on to something important.

Imposter syndrome is different from the nervousness a speaker feels before facing an audience, a temporary insecurity that passes. According to Dr Valerie Young, a psychologist who leads workshops on this syndrome, the imposter doesn't operate this way. No matter how well the speaker does, or how loud the applause, the 'imposter' part always doubts and believes that they could have done better or believes that they just got lucky. Imposter syndrome is the feeling that you are a fraud, despite all evidence to the contrary [1].

Oddly enough, the more successful the 'imposter', the greater the inner stress. It is more common among high achievers. 'It has been called the curse of smart people', because the smarter you are, the more you doubt yourself. Certain kinds of success can come with handcuffs. Each decision you make has to be perfect.' Interestingly, real imposters never suffer from these feelings. Nor do people who are struggling to survive have the luxury of ruminating in such thoughts. One does not imagine the bus driver thinking, 'I have been driving these roads for years, but I am actually a fake' [2].

So how does this feeling come up?

For Michelle Obama, this feeling stemmed from an incident in her youth. Speaking at a London school, Obama recalled how she first experienced the feeling when her school counsellor told her she wasn't 'Princeton material'. She recalls the feeling of being blocked, a feeling she didn't feel for herself.

Obama did make it to Princeton, but she never forgot her counsellor's words and felt that she had a stigma in her own mind. 'I had to overcome the question "am I good enough?"' She believes that hard work is the way to overcome the feelings of self-doubts. She felt like she had something to prove because of her humble background. Despite her success the words of her counsellor left a lasting impression on her adult life.

The words that are communicated in our youth are important in the way we feel about ourselves. The judgement of someone senior to us can affect our self-esteem and our perspectives will be coloured by that lens. Will it scar us, or instead, positively motivate us? Do we feel shame or resilience to succeed? The effect depends on us, on how we choose to react.

## THE GENDER GAP

As we've noted, successful women are more prone to imposter syndrome than are men [3].

Psychologists conclude that differences stem from gender conditioning. They propose that 'success' in countries like the USA has been defined in conventional terms for men rather than women. Historically, ideas of success have often referenced notions such as status, political power and resources. When we think of 'successful women', we don't really think of mums who are taking care of kids and the elderly, or we don't calculate in monetary terms how much friends help friends in need. Any kind of intangible improvement in other people's lives is not counted as successful inputs to society. Often, we find many neighbours who volunteer for the common good of the neighbourhood. In the context of gender conditioning, 'successful women' tends to refer to CEOs of major corporations, politicians and leaders in their respective fields. However, the researchers point out, too, that success usually does not come easily for anyone, male or female [4].

In the book *The Confidence Code*, Katty Kay and Claire Shipman suggest that the rough-and-tumble ways in which boys interact with each other are commonly different from the ways in which girls do.

> With all of their roughhousing and teasing, boys also toughen each other in ways that are actually useful for building resilience. Where many women seek out praise and run from criticism, men usually seem unfazed, able to discount other people's views much earlier in life. [5]

The imposter syndrome can affect even stars we might otherwise think have everything in place. Academy Award winning actress, Kate Winslet, has been quoted: 'I'd wake up in the morning before going off to a shoot, and think, I can't do this; I'm a fraud.' Facebook executive and author of the bestselling book *Lean In*, Sheryl Sandberg has also said she has felt the same way [6].

No doubt, in life we will face rejection, criticism and disappointments, what happens next is up to us. Do we draw back and resign or take the reins and learn? Having the courage to stand up for ourselves and to credit our abilities is part of the process of developing an attitude of worth. If you are among those who have trouble accepting yourself for who you are, bear in mind that you are not alone. Thousands of others carry this burden, and often it is their secret burden that others cannot see.

## Chapter 3: Imposter Syndrome

Being able to trust oneself—a phrase that already suggests an odd relationship between oneself and oneself—is so basic that it is almost always left unarticulated in the background [7].

Imposter syndrome implies, to an extent, that we do not trust our own abilities. It is not just a lack of confidence but an underestimation and deprecation of achievements.

Melanie Patching dreamed of being a professional writer. She knew she enjoyed it and was good at it, but it took a while for her to work up the courage to even apply for a writing job. So when she got hired as a writer at an agency, Melanie was thrilled, but also nervous. She kept doubting her skills, even though no one around her was. After a few years at the agency, she was highly proficient and had been promoted several times. Yet she still behaved like she did on her first day—going far and above her job description to prove herself, helping other colleagues, initiating extra projects, basically being the star student. 'I couldn't just stick to my job description like everyone else was doing, because I felt it wasn't enough. I couldn't shake this underlying fear that I could be found out as a fraud and fired at any moment. I valued my work and really didn't want that to happen. So I overcompensated.'

Further down the line, Melanie wanted a raise. But her imposter syndrome prevented her from directly asking for one. 'I thought I needed to show why I deserved a raise first, so I upped my game even more, taking on two roles at once, going full out, hoping it would end in a raise.' When she did finally ask for one, the answer was no. Her boss was very grateful for the extra work but hadn't actually commissioned it. 'I watched videos on YouTube about asking for a raise and learned that the best strategy is to ask first (before taking on extra responsibilities), promise more results, then follow through and deliver. I asked male friends of mine and some said they asked for a raise (and got one) every six months! I was shocked. I'd done it all wrong because I thought I had to prove myself first.'

She didn't make that mistake again. At her next job, Melanie successfully negotiated a higher salary for her contract, with a raise after probation written in. When asked about what helped her get over her imposter syndrome and have more confidence in herself and what she was worth, she laughed. 'I don't think the fear of being a fraud will ever go away. It will always be there, but that's okay, because it pushes me to be really good at what I do. I think things through, I double check everything, and that means I produce good quality work. But when the fear gets to the point where it feels crippling, I remember what Po's dad said in one of my favourite movies, *Kungfu Panda*: "There is no special ingredient"' [8]. We are all capable in our own unique way.

In 2014, Claire Shipman, a reporter for ABC News, and Katty Kay, the anchor of BBC World News America interviewed some of the most influential women in the USA. They were surprised to find that these people, who, one would assume, would be brimming with confidence, were often crippled by self-doubt [9].

They discovered that compared with men, women don't consider themselves as ready for promotions. They even predict they do worse on tests, and they generally underestimate their abilities. This disparity stems from factors ranging from upbringing to biology.

*Men Are from Mars and Women Are from Venus*, the 1992 bestseller by John Gray was scoffed at by many and taken as dogma by others. His book did carry some truth in its observation that women seek to share, while men seek to fix. In broad terms, women are articulators, while men are doers: When a woman hurts, she wants to open up about it. When a man hurts, he wants to locate the problem and resolve it. Although many people take the stance that differences between men and women should not be exaggerated, differences like these can be important. Perhaps the 'fix-it' orientation of many men is part of what adds to self-confidence over time.

Brenda Major, a social psychologist at the University of California, studied this problem of self-perception decades ago. She set up tests where she would ask men and women how they thought they were going to do on a variety of tasks. She found that the men consistently overestimated their abilities and subsequent performance, and that the women routinely underestimated both. The actual performances did not differ in quality. She felt that these findings have been consistent and are relevant even today [10].

Men do struggle with self-doubt, but not as intensely and commonly as women do. The interesting fact is that men less frequently let their doubts stop them from moving towards a goal. In some instances, there is even a tendency towards overconfidence. This can happen quite naturally. Ernesto Reuben, a professor at Columbia Business School, has come up with a term for this phenomenon—honest overconfidence [11].

MaryAnn Voli is a Hong Kong based executive coach, leadership development expert and mindfulness teacher [12]. She agrees that men suffer from imposter syndrome too. Theirs is often a result of comparisons with others in terms of their education, social status or cultural background. If a man studied in a less than recognizable university, he may feel unworthy compared to someone who attended Harvard or MIT. Those from a working-class background feel inferior to the so-called 'elite' class. Voli says that one must understand that these kinds of thoughts affect office morale. If the negative thoughts persist, it is important to counter the imposter statements with positive truths. Beliefs may be ingrained, but that does not mean they are fixed. On the contrary, one's internal stories can be edited constantly. 'Where attention goes, energy flows', Voli says. When the intensity of a rigid corporate culture breaks down your self-confidence, accept your feelings and your pain, then move ahead with resolve. Don't say 'I shouldn't feel this way'.

The 'shouldn't' does not help in curbing feelings. Bad feelings will come, let them come, but don't dwell on them, turn your attention elsewhere.

Voli has worked with many executives and business leaders. She feels that there is a general tendency in the corporate world to project a vibe of invincibility. 'No one likes to use the word "weaknesses" but prefer to use words like "developmental" to define an organization's weak spot. The executives tiptoe around these words, as if by saying it they will decline.'

The imposter syndrome persists in the corporate world predominantly because of the impulse to outshine others and to hide weaknesses. When a feeling of self-doubt starts to affect one's mindset, then one must step back and focus on the positive, advises Voli. 'Remember why you were hired, what your strengths are and why you are successful. If you are still affected, then you can make choices to leave the toxic workplace. You can white knuckle it and admit that this place is not for you. Then decide what can be done. Focus on other positive areas in your life—family, hobbies, friendships, spiritual connections.'

She noted that in the last two years, there has been a positive transformation in many corporate cultures. They have moved to a more human-centric leadership model. But if the company has a rainmaker, someone on whom the survival of the business depends, the higher ups will be unlikely to challenge them, even if they cause others misery.

## ACADEMIC ANGST

Imposter syndrome is also found in universities among the more cerebral and intellectual. Many of the most respected academics in the world are certain that they are not worthy of their position, that they are faking it and that they will soon be found out. These sentiments can be found at every

## Chapter 3: Imposter Syndrome

level. The pressure and the competitive environment fill many academics with self-doubt regarding their abilities and qualifications.

Eliza is a PhD student working in the biochemistry department of the University of Toronto, Canada. She says, 'I just didn't realize the way I felt had a name. It's literally the feeling that you're not good enough and you don't deserve to be at the table. Most of the time I manage it well, but sometimes this crippling self-doubt and insecurity gets to me.'

According to Eliza, it is ridiculously common. 'At least one professor I know has imposter syndrome and lots of graduate students and post doctorates have it too.' She goes on to share that they all face mental health strain, which she attributes to the ultracompetitive culture [13].

Comparison is at the heart of impostor syndrome and, as the saying goes, comparison is the thief of joy.

In India, Amrita Mahale studied as the lone woman in her engineering class in IIT and she even wrote about female students experiencing the imposter syndrome in classes that are dominated by men. Mahale says that when she introduces herself as a rocket scientist, she is not joking. She studied aeronautical engineering both in college and graduate school. When asked why she's no longer a rocket scientist, her responses range from graceful—'I was fascinated by flight, by the poetic idea of overreaching and escape'—to witty—'Studying aeronautics because you are fascinated by flight is like becoming a gynaecologist because you like watching porn.' Her sense of humour is admirable but what it really conveys is her self-doubt. She was made to feel that she was not good enough. 'To have a meaningful career as a researcher in science or engineering one had to be a genius, but I thought I was only an aberration.' In school and college in India, Mahale was under crushing pressure to prove she was worthy.

'It was in graduate school in the USA that I learnt about the impostor syndrome, a psychological pattern where one believes, in spite of evidence to the contrary, that one is a fraud, that one's successes are sheer flukes. Imposter syndrome, huh, I remember thinking. Trust the Americans to come up with big names for the weight of bad decisions, like the decision to pursue science or engineering when one is not cut out for it.' Mahale returned to India and pursued a different career path.

The number of women scientists in India is low in proportion to women who study science. The All India Survey on Higher Education 2017–2018 estimates that 40 per cent of the undergraduates in science and engineering are women, but women make up only 14 per cent of scientists, engineers and technologists employed in research and development institutions [14].

In addition, number of women scientists publishing their work in research journals is also low [15].

## INTERLINKED WITH SELF-ESTEEM

There is another hindrance in the culture of education in India. In a column in the *Times of India*, Devashish Chakravarty, CEO of QuezX.com and HeadHonchos.com, a recruitment agency and career services platform, says that in India it is common for education and initial career choices to be made by elders or even by the individual's peers [16].

Who knows? Having imposter syndrome could make someone even more dependent on those who impose their decisions.

A study found that low self-esteem and imposter syndrome are intertwined in that people with low self-esteem are particularly vulnerable. What this means in practical terms is that if we want to overcome imposter syndrome, we must be prepared to question its narratives in our mind just as we would question narratives that give us low self-esteem [17].

Dr Fredric Neuman, a New York based psychiatry specialist and author, explains that changing ingrained ideas is very difficult. Some people with low self-esteem continue to feel bad about themselves despite their successes in the world. Although their accomplishments are clear and everyone thinks well of them, they feel that they will be asked to do something beyond their abilities. The world will see, then, that they have been 'faking it' [18].

Simon Squibb is a serial entrepreneur. He is on a mission to help one million people start their own businesses. He is no stranger to the syndrome. 'When I was 15 and started a company, I felt I was not really an entrepreneur and more a kid trying to be an entrepreneur. I just kept going. As an adult, I started to invest in start-ups, many big-name investment firms and those investing from large firms. During those years, I always felt people looked at me and said "he is not a real investor, he is only investing small amounts of money in companies compared to us."'

Their words affected Simon. He felt like he didn't fit in and was an imposter. Simon is a resilient man, so he chooses not to let the critics affect his self-belief. He works from a place of sincerity and authenticity. 'I'm sometimes a small fish in a big pond and other times a big fish in a small pond and I never make anyone else feel like an imposter. I try to control my own feelings by realizing we all have to start somewhere.'

Simon has started over 17 businesses, invested in 66 and has mentored hundreds of founders. He sold his digital agency to a large company and now focuses on inspiring, motivating and guiding budding and experienced entrepreneurs through his podcast. Simon accepts that he is not a Joe Rogan with millions of fans and, therefore, is aware that the imposter syndrome may creep up on him. 'I just take a deep breath, focus less on others who are perhaps bigger than me and my show, and focus on doing my show well and getting better at it. One day I will get there and not feel like an imposter. I know that it just takes time and patience' [19].

These professionals are confronting the imposter syndrome head-on by questioning the negative stories that it propagates. In so doing, we can have greater hope for happiness and growth at work. But the imposter syndrome can also emerge outside work, in our personal relationships.

## IMPERFECT RELATIONSHIPS

The search for love seems to be universal. It is one of the basic ingredients of wellness. But do we recognize the importance of self-love? Erich Fromm, noted psychologist, points out that love is an 'art form that takes dedication and practice, not something you fall into. It is a faculty to be developed, one that begins with learning to love yourself'. Faith in yourself enables you to face challenges and failures without falling into the trap of worry and judgement. And you become less dependent on the validation and reassurance of others.

Valentina Tudose is a clinical hypnotherapist and a relationship coach [20]. She says that in the old days, love was simpler to understand and so were relationships. She didn't grow up in what she calls a 'Disneyfied' expectation of love. It seems that the way people approach relationship involves high expectations and a 'happily ever after' mentality. This false belief is based on fairy-tale romances. You cannot assume such a romance will be any more permanent than the roller coaster emotions that it is based on. As time passes and partners grow, they transform and sometimes in surprising ways. 'Everyone has issues these days. They are constantly struggling to deal with them in an environment that conditions our beliefs to expect too much or ask for too little. We are told how to feel, how to think and to follow a rulebook on dating. This is social programming. We are conditioned by old beliefs, our upbringing and environment.'

Tudose believes that there are two paths that people generally tend to follow in life: the victim path and the hero path. To speak of the victim path is not to deny that at times life has injustices. Of course, the world is filled with ups and downs. Humans manifest a combination of good and evil. At times, we will find ourselves on the wrong end of the stick, victims of others' maltreatment. When Tudose speaks of the victim path, however, she is not describing these very real and painful experiences.

The victim blames his/her environment and external factors for his/her problems. He or she takes the passive approach to life. Any disadvantages in life are blamed on a person's destiny or other people. The individual never looks within, never tries to change himself or herself. The hero, on the other hand, chooses to make the best of his or her situation. Even when heroes face challenges, they are proactive in finding creative ways to achieve their goals. This means they have the ability to overcome their own sense of doubt, inadequacies and fear.

What do these factors have to do with imposter syndrome in a relationship? Tudose says that it involves a certain way of managing relationships. If things are going well, those afflicted with the syndrome suddenly feel that there's something wrong and they will soon be found out to be 'imperfect'.

Most of Tudose's clients are extremely confident in their workplace, skilled in managing a team and making executive decisions, but for some reason falter in relationships.

One such client, Mingmei, a Chinese 47-year-old successful executive, came to Tudose for help. She was in a perfect relationship with a French man, Louis, but was finding it hard to understand why she didn't want to commit to Louis. Mingmei is from an ethnic Chinese background. In her culture, any woman over the age of 35 didn't stand a chance to find an eligible Chinese man. Before she met Louis, Mingmei decided to expand her pool of choices and wanted to marry before she turned 48. Apparently, Mingmei's Feng Shui master had predicted that after the age of 48, she had no chance of marriage. In a desperate rush to find Mr Right, she signed up with dating and meet-up groups before she finally met Louis. They hit it off so well that they felt like they were soulmates. But a lingering thought in Mingmei's mind had taken root: What if she was not good enough for him. The fear gripped her, and she confided in Tudose, 'This relationship is too good to be true'.

Mingmei was thinking of ending their relationship—not because it was going badly, but because it seemed 'too good'. Mingmei felt she was not good enough for this amazing person and that he deserved a younger woman. She felt like a fraud and was wracked with self-doubt.

This self-sabotaging behaviour was affecting how she viewed herself. She had grown up believing that struggle to achieve or get the 'sweet fruit' is part of life. And when things go well, it must be a mirage or an illusion. It seems that Mingmei was stuck in this vicious cycle of self-doubt. 'He deserves so much better, and every second that he spends with me means a missed opportunity to meet a truly wonderful woman who would make him happier.' She felt guilty.

Tudose discovered that when Mingmei was going through her imposter phase, Louis would praise her, calm her feelings, but even though she accepted the compliments, she would doubt his words. With Tudose's coaching, Mingmei slowly began to realize that she was having irrational thoughts, founded on a belief system that was from her youth. Mingmei had received a perfect opportunity for love and was turning it down. She began to question her own doubts and eventually was able to find a balance within herself, a sense of self-acceptance that she deserved happiness, and that she was valued and loved.

Tudose explains that at the root of a relationship imposter syndrome is low self-esteem. 'When Mingmei felt that she wasn't good enough for her partner, it indicates a gap between how others perceive her and how she perceives herself.'

Tudose gives the account of another client Brenda, who felt unworthy of marriage. Brenda had extremely low self-esteem. She told Tudose that she was treated like a loser all her life and her parents were harsh critics and stingy with praise. Brenda felt inferior to everyone she met. And projecting that feeling affected how people treated her. Her sense of worthlessness was slowly destroying her.

Tudose pointed out that a lot of our emotional baggage stems from childhood. Through hypnotherapy, Tudose was able to help Brenda heal her trauma. As a result, she has been able to change habits and beliefs which are all stored in the subconscious. 'We don't realize how strongly our decisions are affected by our beliefs stuck since our childhood.'

When people have imposter syndrome, they are slow to internalize accomplishments, but quick to see themselves through the lens of failure. They might be very successful and even might overachieve on a regular basis. And yet, the negative voice inside can be very sinister. Deep down, they may feel scared of being unmasked anytime.

## TYPES OF IMPOSTER SYNDROME

Dr Valerie Young is an internationally recognized expert on imposter syndrome. She explains that this syndrome goes beyond a mere lack of confidence. Everyone experiences bouts of self-doubt from time to time, especially when attempting something new. But because the imposter voice inside us has insanely high self-expectations, the self-doubt is chronic. Despite multiple awards, accolades and achievements, rather than congratulate themselves, the person will put their success down to luck, timing or even an error in judgement from their employer.

This failure to accept one's own accomplishments can prove problematic, especially when it is time to strive to make major career strides. If you're continually fearful you don't measure up, you'll find it difficult to make the most of your potential, or you may hesitate to put yourself forward for a position or promotion that you really deserve.

Dr Young's findings revealed that because people who feel like imposters hold themselves to an unrealistic and unsustainable standard of competence, falling short of this standard evokes shame. She has confirmed this with people from all walks of life and all phases of their careers.

However, a further in-depth research revealed that imposters don't all experience failure-related shame the same way. And the reason is that they don't all define competence in the same way.

Dr Young offers the following five types of imposters based on how competence is understood.

- The perfectionist believes if there's any flaw, it's ruined.
- The expert believes if you don't know it *all*, then you're a failure.
- The soloist believes they must accomplish any task alone for it to count as success.
- The natural genius believes any struggle felt in learning new skills or handling different tasks is shameful.
- The superhuman believes they must perform all the roles in their professional and personal life, perfectly, or they don't measure up.

Dr Young says that changing the way one feels is difficult but changing our thought processes helps in overcoming this inner conflict [21].

Compassionately challenging one's own feelings of lack of confidence can be a healthy way to increase one's sense of wholeness over time. However, this is not to say that overconfidence is a virtue. In fact, it can cause its own problems. The stock market is an arena where many researchers have shown clear evidence of the tendency of overconfidence to cause people to make mistakes.

Excessive and unjustified confidence can actually lead to ruinous investment behaviour, according to a recent study by Money Crashers, a service that educates on financial matters. It cites a study from the University of California, Berkeley, which states that men are more prone to display this weakness of overconfidence. The point is not to characterize all men—clearly all individuals differ. The point is to know about tendencies in the workplace. In the study, men were twice as likely as women to report that their returns beat the broader US market. In social psychology, this is known as illusory superiority. It is illusory because it's mathematically impossible for most people to literally be above average. And research has shown that this bias can lead to potentially destructive investment behaviour [22].

## ILLUSORY SUPERIORITY

Thus far we have considered what it is like to suffer from imposter syndrome. Some readers might say that it doesn't apply to their personality profile or that they even suffer from tendencies quite opposite in nature. It is useful, then, to consider what such opposite tendencies might look like in a specific example.

Maj. Gen. Neeraj Bali (Retd) runs a consultancy for businesses. 'In my experience, the critical attribute that makes all the difference to the collective psychological well-being in a company—indeed in any organization—is the prevalence of a deleterious culture. Culture is what casts the longest possible shadow on all affairs. And while its manifestations are visible, the strong stream of culture flows just beneath the surface, dragging everyone with it.' He shares a case study [23].

Srinivasan Murali is a self-made man. He didn't linger in the college for too long and took a plunge into the world of entrepreneurship. He had a laser-like focus, and his company grew from a small shop of 6 employees to a mid-sized company of over 2,000 professionals. The company, a supplier of electrical and electronic material for significant infrastructure projects, developed a footprint right across India. Within two decades of existence, he was already harbouring notions of going public and negotiating for contracts abroad.

But something was amiss. No matter how hard Srinivasan tried, the company refused to rise above a certain level, as measured by the revenue and profitability. It appeared that the whole system was creaking. He was good at securing new business, but delivery was increasingly becoming an issue.

'Our growth has become our biggest challenge', he once remarked, arguably the wisest statement he had ever made.

He had spotted the problem well. He also knew that the problem lay in the existence of poor processes and procedures. You can run a small enterprise by macromanaging it, but for a bigger ship, you need processes in place that will steer it in the right direction. He pushed his top leadership to create and enforce rules. He hummed, and he hawed. But the elephant refused to budge.

Finally, he fell back on to the stratagem that most companies do when problems appear intractable—a consulting firm was hired at great expense.

Six months later, the consultants were ready with their answers. But there was a problem. The analysis and the solution were not likely to be palatable to the managing director, Srinivasan Murali. They had concluded that he was the problem.

How so?

It appeared that Srinivasan clearly suffered from a severe case of low esteem. This manifested in many ways. He was deeply suspicious that if he did not have a ring of 'spies', his employees will perform below par or, worse, their machinations would lead to serious losses. The people who derived benefit from this dispensation were mostly self-serving and inefficient employees who would routinely carry unsubstantiated gossip to Srinivasan. And, armed with the knowledge, he always cribbed and cursed about the imaginary offenders to others—his own brother, who was the vice-president, being one of the receivers of this mischievous gossip. And the word got back to the victims—invariably hardworking professionals who would refuse to stoop to such tactics. The demoralising effect was evident.

He could also not let go of the tendency to micromanage. 'I have to do everything because no one else will' was a lament many had heard from him. That statement was factually wrong. He was only giving counsel to his low self-esteem by dealing with mid- or junior-level managers, almost as if he wanted their approval and to spread the popularity of his 'leadership'. Those who thus had his ear used it to undercut their immediate superiors. Why bother about your reporting officer when you are dealing with the managing director, the man who has to decide bonuses and pay rise at the end of the year? The impact on the motivation of senior leadership was obvious. The morale dipped, and people worked for the salary. Ownership was conspicuous by absence.

Srinivasan could not bring himself to appreciate others. He feared, perhaps, that it would raise people's expectations of the end-of-the-year raise. He was a father in competition with his children.

Then there was also the issue of the quality of new intake. After all the expression of intention to make the company a truly modern one, he invariably favoured new entrants who may be good at the craft but were decidedly less than articulate and somewhat weak in the intellect department. He didn't want anyone to be superior to himself—the king—in any form or shape.

How could then the company move forward? The change had to be initiated at the very top, and the steps had to be radical. Who will tell him that it was his low-esteem make-up that was the enemy?

The consultants made a valiant effort. They first tried to have a one-on-one sitting with him. But he insisted on a wider audience, clearly unmindful of the fact of what lay ahead. The presentation was diplomatically worded, but there was no way to put so much gloss on the findings that the blow could be softened. As it progressed, Srinivasan began to pick holes in the methodology adopted by the consultants. Gradually, he started expressing disappointment at having 'paid them so much'. The audience had little choice to not only agree with him but to reinforce his criticism. Who will tell the truth to someone who wants to hear a lie and hold the pen of authority in his hand? This was a truck headed for the cliff.

By the end of the day, the consultants were fired.

Is there an easy answer to such a problem? Of course, there isn't. The change has to begin with whosoever is suffering from low esteem. But the central challenge is that people with low self-esteem are least likely to acknowledge it to anyone, leave alone seek help. They need the help the most.

And they are the biggest thorn-laced obstacle in the possibility of growth and change.

What Srinivasan was experiencing is what some psychologists call the Dunning–Kruger effect, which refers to the tendency to overestimate one's capabilities. Srinivasan may have been capable in business, but he lacked the ability to manage a team. He was overconfident.

When a person suffers from this sort of illusory superiority, it is a form of cognitive bias. The person overestimates their own competence relative to others. Interestingly, since the person overrates himself or herself, it is the mirror opposite of imposter syndrome [24].

Why is illusory superiority important in a discussion of imposter syndrome? Well, it is useful for a few reasons. First, whether you suffer from imposter syndrome or illusory superiority, it is useful for anyone to be aware of the remarkable diversity of personality styles. Are you shocked by the fact that someone who is quite the opposite from you operates in your life space? Shocked or not, these remarkable differences exist. The sooner you come to terms with this, better equipped you are to manage problems that arise.

In another way of thinking, perhaps we can learn from our opposites. Of course, it would be useless to swing from one extreme to another. Perhaps persons who are inclined to overlook their own strengths and achievements can take a page from colleagues who are comfortably aware of their capabilities. And perhaps those who suffer an inflated sense of their performance can learn from the example offered by their more reticent and humble peers.

When we struggle with internal doubt, a personal problem with ourselves, there is no person or job that can make us feel good in the long run. We fundamentally don't feel good enough, no matter how much evidence proves otherwise. Only when we realize this can we change.

Beliefs are not facts; they are not set in stone. We can change the way we think about ourselves as much as we can change how we perceive others. Overcoming imposter syndrome requires self-acceptance: one doesn't need to attain perfection or mastery to be worthy of the success. Nor is it about lowering the bar, it is about resetting it to a realistic level that doesn't leave one feeling inadequate and forever overreaching.

## BOTTOM LINE

So what do the experts say we can do about imposter syndrome? Dr Jessamy Hibberd, clinical psychologist and author of *The Imposter Cure*, offers several strategies to help us become clearer and confident [25].

It is important to realize that you can enjoy your success without the old fears holding you back. An example of this is being able to be humble and courageous without the anxiety of imposter feelings. She suggests reflection, which helps to refine our thoughts, evaluate our capabilities and set realistic goals. We learn much more from our experiences when we reflect on what we've done. Making notes helps to gain new perspectives and consider an alternative way of thinking about yourself and your achievements. It enables you to look back and see how you are doing.

Imposter is not what pushes you or makes you good at what you do; you are the one that does this.

## REFERENCES

1. Abrams A. Yes, impostor syndrome is real: here's how to deal with it. Time; 2018 June 20. Available from: http://www.time.com/5312483/how-to-deal-with-impostor-syndrome/
2. Bhargava S. The imposter syndrome: feeling like a fraud. The Financial Express; 2003 April 12. Available from: https://www.financialexpress.com/archive/the-imposter-syndrome-feeling-like-a-fraud/76569/
3. Burch RL. Things are not what they seem. Evol Psychol 2020;8(1). Available from: https://doi.org/10.1177/147470491000800112
4. Kanazawa S, Perina K. Why do so many women experience the 'imposter syndrome'? Psychology Today; 2009. Available from: https://www.psychologytoday.com/intl/blog/the-scientific-fundamentalist/200912/why-do-so-many-women-experience-the-imposter-syndrome
5. Kay K, Shipman C. The confidence code: the science and art of self-assurance—what women should know. New York, NY: HarperCollins; 2018. p. 91.

6. Wessel R. Feel like a fraud? You're not alone. BBC; 2015. Available from: https://www.bbc.com/worklife/article/20150916-feel-like-a-fraud-youre-not-alone
7. Solomon RC, Flores F. Building trust in business, politics, relationships, and life. New York, NY: Oxford University Press; 2003.
8. Patching M. Zoom interview. Hong Kong; 2020 July 17.
9. Kay K, Shipman C. The confidence gap. The Atlantic; 2014 April 15. Available from: https://www.theatlantic.com/magazine/archive/2014/05/the-confidence-gap/359815/
10. Eccleston C, Major B. Attributions to discrimination and self-esteem: The role of group identification and appraisals. Group Process Intergroup Relat. 2006;9(2):147–162. Available from: https://doi.org/10.1177/1368430206062074
11. Utah State University. Overconfident men. Utah State University; 2015. Available from: https://www.usu.edu/uwlp/blog/2015/overconfident-men
12. Voli M. Zoom interview. Portugal; 2020 July 15.
13. Eliza. Phone chat. UK; 2020 July 7.
14. Mhale A. Women in science are made to feel like impostors. Hindustan Times; 2019 January 2. Available from: https://www.hindustantimes.com/analysis/women-in-science-are-made-to-feel-like-impostors/story-odOJ1VnpPJbeZAeIDcM0LI.html
15. Kulkarni R. Gender inequality uniformly high in Indian academic publishing. The Wire Science; 2019 February 24. Available from: https://science.thewire.in/society/gender/women/gender-inequality-uniformly-high-in-indian-academic-publishing/

16. Chakravarty D. Do you lack confidence in your abilities at work? Try these 6 steps. The Economic Times; n.d. Available from https://economictimes.indiatimes.com/wealth/earn/do-you-lack-confidence-in-your-abilities-at-work-try-these-6-steps/articleshow/71770279.cms?from=mdr

17. Schubert N, Bowker A. Examining the impostor phenomenon in relation to self-esteem level and self-esteem instability. Curr. Psychol. 2017. Available from: https://doi.org/10.1007/s12144-017-9650-4

18. Neuman F. Low self-esteem. Psychology Today; 2013. Available from: https://www.psychologytoday.com/us/blog/fighting-fear/201304/low-self-esteem

19. Squibb S. Email interview. Hong Kong; 2020 July 15.

20. Tudose V. Face-to-face interview. Hong Kong; 2020 July 10.

21. Young V. The 5 types of impostors. Impostor Syndrome; 2011 December 6. https://impostorsyndrome.com/5-types-of-impostors/

22. Money Crashers. Men vs. women—how the sexes differ in their psychology of investing (survey). Money Crashers; n.d. Available from: https://www.moneycrashers.com/men-vs-women-psychology-investing/

23. Bali N. Email. Delhi; 2020 July 30.

24. Beaumord C. The opposite of imposter syndrome is just as harmful. Medium; 2019 August 2. Available from: https://creatheory.com/the-opposite-of-imposter-syndrome-is-just-as-harmful-b8328510f021

25. Hibberd J. The imposter cure: how to stop feeling like a fraud and escape the mind-trap of imposter syndrome. London: Hachette UK; 2019.

We all have cluttered cobwebbed parts of our minds which need our attention. Past memories, ones we wish we could completely erase, can haunt us for decades. These negative reflections may come with shame and guilt, layered with regrets. Our hearts cower with fear. When our past triggers such emotions, the body reacts defensively and we wonder why we feel drained. This is the time to address memories that block our forward progress. We must face them with courage, acknowledge their existence—no matter how painful—and let them go. And we must let go of toxic 'isms': criticism, judgementalism and perfectionism for a clear mental path forward. When we do this, we can let go of our constant need to feel 'good enough' to prove our worth, to validate our existence.

This is the time for self-care. Embrace your younger self. Forgive yourself and others. Recognize the truth of your own uniqueness.

Reflect regularly, mainly to audit, and let go of many conditioned beliefs. In this phase of your life, rediscover your inner strengths, your raison d'etre. Make peace with the background chatter: the 'what ifs'. Question it if need be. But don't succumb to the voice that weakens you.

At times, we neglect our own views and become a follower instead of a leader. It happens to the best of us when we doubt ourselves. Childhood conditioning may have weakened our self-trust. But phantoms of our past don't need to stop us from achieving our full potential. Overcoming those preconditioned responses is necessary to find clarity and understand what works best for us. If we are alert in moments of weakness, we will be prepared to rise above oppressive feelings.

As humans, it is in our nature to tap into our inner and outer worlds. We are made more complicated by social norms and cultural traditions. Yet we are unique creatures capable of adapting to a world that is changing at breakneck speed. Let us not fail at it.

# CHAPTER 4

# BIG TALK SMALL TALK

*Self-criticism, like self-administered brain surgery, is perhaps not a good idea. Can the 'self' see the 'self' with any objectivity?*

—Joyce Carol Oates

## VERSIONS OF SELF

What we believe to be true has been fed to us from childhood to adulthood. We are influenced in schools and universities, and again in the workplace. Without examining these ingested beliefs, we accept them as truth, even in adulthood. Such unquestioned beliefs become our unexamined internal stories. They are frequently not based on solid facts. But regardless of whether they are true, they can affect our feelings, commitments and goals.

'We are the only species that can believe in ourselves, lie to ourselves, convince ourselves, love or hate ourselves, accept ourselves, push and pull ourselves', says Chris Biebauer in his book *No Self, No Problem: How Neuropsychology Is Catching up to Buddhism*. When we base our life on a belief system that involves 'not being good enough', we experience emotions that affect our sense of self. These internal stories can be confining rather than liberating. If we care too much about what others think, we become dependent. This voice has little to do with logic. If we believe we are useless, then we pay a cost in terms of our energy and focus.

When we talk about communication, we normally think about it in relation to everyone else. It is true that how others speak with us can impact us significantly. Imagine having a bully for a boss!

Honda, the global car-making giant, was established in 1946. Its expansion has been from a small wooden shack making bicycles to the multinational automobile and motorcycle manufacturer we all know today. The founder Soichiro Honda was praised and recognized for his great achievements in engineering. The American Society of Mechanical Engineers established the Soichiro Honda Medal. Honda was also inducted into the Automotive Hall of Fame in 1989.

Soichiro Honda was also known to be an exacting boss. In a recent business article, a former executive recalled: 'When he got mad, he blindly reached for anything lying around and start throwing randomly at people' [1].

Not just Japan but globally such fiery tempers are common among managers, it seems. A Japanese psychologist even coined a term to describe this particular abuse: *pawahara* or power harassment. Japanese's labour ministry defines six categories of power harassment: physical attacks, mental attacks, social isolation, excessive demands, demeaning demands and privacy infringement.

It is too frequently a problem. But the bigger part of the problem is how a powerful personality, a senior, a person we look up to with respect, can affect our inner talk.

We talk to ourselves internally, and this is an issue that many people don't pay attention to. From the moment we wake up until we go to sleep, we are subject to our internal dialogue which helps us to navigate through our day. Our feelings and actions are connected to this voice.

If our thoughts determine how we feel, that means how we habitually think will determine how we habitually feel, says Nick Wignall, a clinical psychologist. Negative self-talk, also known as cognitive distortions, is usually inaccurate and leads to negative emotions. So if we want to change how we feel, we must first learn to change how we think [2].

Jonathan Heston tells us in his book, *The Unlimited Self: Destroy Limiting Beliefs, Uncover Inner Greatness, and Live the Good Life,* that we have not been taught how to deal with our thoughts and the inner voice. Our thoughts are not our identity, but we assume they are. Without thinking about it, we define ourselves by what we think, and this can be a burden.

Hong Kong Confidential is an entertaining podcast created by Australian-born Jules Hannaford. She interviews amazing people about their lives, personal journeys and secrets. Jules is also the author of *Fool Me Twice*, which details the dangers and pitfalls she experienced in her search for love online. She grew up in rural South Australia before moving to Adelaide, the state's capital city, where she started her career as a teacher.

When Jules was in her twenties, she was in an abusive relationship with a man from another country. They dated and married three years later. Jules hoped that Gustav would be different after they settled into family life, but unfortunately, he did not. He would call her names and make her feel guilty for the smallest problem. 'He used to call me stupid all the time. He would say that I would never amount to anything in my career. It is amazing how when somebody repeatedly calls you stupid and dumb, then you start to believe them.' He was physically and emotionally violent. He used to scream and yell at her and smash things around her. However, Jules was in love with him, so she tried to carry on, hoping he would change.

She knew that when he spoke and behaved aggressively this was unacceptable, but she didn't have the courage or the wherewithal to take a stand against him. 'The smallest problem would set him off.... His behaviour was very cyclical; we would fight, he would eventually apologise, we would make up and then the pattern would start again. There was a lot of gaslighting and coercive control in our relationship. I didn't understand the meaning of those terms at that time. Looking back, I can see that I was being emotionally abused constantly.'

When she became pregnant, she was initially thrilled, but her husband was not happy as he did not want to have children. During the pregnancy, her mother witnessed Gustav's violent behaviour. Her mother suggested that Jules should leave him, but Jules was convinced that after the birth of her baby, her husband would turn over a new leaf. She stayed with Gustav, continued to study and manage her home. Jules only missed three weeks of university when her daughter was born.

'It was all very gradual, but I was losing my own identity. It was in the last two years of our marriage that things got worse.... I lost touch with reality. It was just Gustav, my baby and my thoughts. My inner voice started to repeat Gustav's words like an echo, and I began to believe them.' Jules finally left her husband when her daughter was ten months old after her parents implored her to leave and offered to help with the move. Once she was free, she felt relieved and liberated. Her family's support made it much easier to manage and get along financially. Jules had great dreams to become a school teacher, and she was determined to achieve her goal. She continued to study and worked nights to make ends meet while her cousin looked after her daughter.

Jules was able to cope but in some ways, her past haunted her. With every life challenge, she second guessed her ability to make good decisions. She didn't trust her judgement at times, and she had many more failed relationships after her disastrous marriage.

Despite the distance, Gustav was a dark shadow that hovered over her. Even over the phone, he was violent and aggressive. When he came to meet their daughter, any slight issue could lead to a temperamental or threatening reaction. After a few years, he gradually lost interest in Jules and their daughter. At that time, it took a lot of courage for Jules to stay strong, but she focussed on her career and tried to give her daughter all the best possible opportunities. The difficult fact was that the abuse she received became part of her thinking, part of her self-talk. I would take time to heal from this.

Now, at age 55, looking back, Jules knows she made the right decision to move away from the abusive relationship. She completed university education and began a successful career. She achieved her goal despite the setbacks and has been a teacher for 30 years. She recalls that in her youth, she had been a confident and extroverted person with a healthy sense of self-esteem. Jules was able to bounce back with the support of family and friends. As a single mother, she was able to live her life on her terms. Her daughter is happy and healthy and lives a wonderful life [3].

Researcher and developmental neuropsychiatrist, Martin H. Teicher notes that verbal abuse is as harmful as physical abuse. Our world, attitudes and behaviour are shaped by the way certain individuals speak to us. It is natural for us to instinctively believe the messages we hear from those we love and trust. But when we are attentive, we can change our way of thinking and our view of the world.

## ROOTED IN CHILDHOOD

Psychologists agree that most children from a young age start to internalize the language they hear from those around them. These are often negative words or prohibitions like, 'Don't talk to strangers', 'Don't talk like that', 'Don't go there' and so on. Initially, the inner voice is a helpful guide, steering us away from potential harm and offering a moral compass for actions.

But later, as the child becomes an adolescent, this inbuilt mechanism becomes more punishing. The individual is overwhelmed by words that preach that he or she is not good enough: 'Nobody really likes you, so you better not risk further humiliation.' This talk clouds one's spirit and mind. The residual negative feeling warns us, 'that hurt—do not repeat!' Neuroscience research tells us that this fear functions in the brain in the same way as a real threat. It reacts in the same way whether a tiger is chasing you or you are bullying yourself [4].

This negativity and pressure can become an automatic habit that extends into adulthood. If we are a perfectionist, expectations of ourselves rise sky high. And even if we are doing great, our inner critic finds fault.

When we feel sensitive, our self-esteem is more vulnerable. It reacts to changing circumstances quickly. When the inner critic is unleashed, it can get harsh. What can be done? The best way forward is to be mindful and then see how to help in a manner that doesn't magnify the doubts and criticism. It must be accomplished by a shift from negative feelings of worthlessness, inferiority and shame to affirming thoughts of compassion, connection and competence. This will enable us to rediscover our sense of intrinsic worth.

## THE PURPOSE OF THE INNER CRITIC

Self-talk is also known as intrapersonal communication, which is the internal use of speech and language. It appears in the form of thoughts that we can 'hear' with the auditory part of the brain. This self-talk goes on all day in different situations. Sometimes we are aware of it and other times, we hear it as a running commentary like a sports commentator commenting as events unfold. Ian Tuhovsky explains in his book *The Science of Self-talk* that there are two kinds of talk: constructive or dysfunctional. Are the words critical or a form of praise? Similarly, self-talk measures our own moment-to-moment performance. It can border from being pleasant to toxic, leading to feelings that can be empowering or crushing.

Constructive talk helps you to move in the right direction like achieving a goal or developing skills. Dysfunctional self-talk, on the other hand, results in an unproductive mindset or feelings of misery and helplessness. Tuhovsky points out that the negative effect is not necessarily the enemy. It is an alert to a situation that needs attention. It need not be demotivational if we take steps to make it useful.

Tara Mohr is a career coach and an expert on women's leadership and well-being. She claims that we have within each of us a 'safety instinct' which uses harsh words. This inner critic tries to protect us and keep us secure. For example, if you want to learn public speaking or share an innovative idea with your boss, you might hear your inner critic saying something like, 'you'll make a fool of yourself' or 'wait until you are more experienced'. This safety instinct is trying to help us avoid harm.

The problem is that everything that brings us the most fulfilment, personally and professionally, always involves taking the kinds of risks that the safety instinct doesn't like. That's why we've got to learn to be aware of the negative inner voice, but not allow it to become our boss.

Some forms of the negative talk are short-lived. They act upon us for a while and then dissipate. Another form of negative talk is more pernicious because it involves repeatedly going over worries and concerns. Psychologists call this rumination. It can lead to depression, anxiety and other severe disorders.

Karishma, a 28-year-old advertising professional, sought therapy as she was dealing with an increased amount of anxiety related to work. She experienced sleepless nights and a sense of dread that she would feel each time she had to attend an important meeting at work. Her problem came to a head when in the middle of conducting a presentation, she found herself going blank, evidently from anxiety. Midway through, she started to feel the room caving in on her, and she froze.

Karishma is a high-achieving individual who always excelled at everything she took on. Her parents were professionals—her father a chartered accountant and her mother a dentist. Growing up, academic performance and participating in co-curricular activities were all-important, unquestioned priorities. Karishma described her childhood as being very goal driven. Good grades on an exam paper were acknowledged, but she had to quickly move on to the next achievement. Her parents were not very liberal with their praise, and their explanation was: 'If you revel too much in this victory, it might get to your head.' With time, the belief that Karishma started to harbour about herself was: 'I am not good or worthy enough unless I achieve this or that.'

In other words, her self-worth was contingent on reaching milestones rather than based on unconditional self-acceptance, which can be a problem [5]. However, no achievement was sufficient for her. She reached a goal, and it was time to unlock the next stage. There was no time to savour the hard work and effort she had put in to get to where she was.

Having completed her MBA from a prestigious business school in India at a fairly young age, Karishma entered the corporate world with a high-paying job as an advertising executive. She found herself in a high-pressure environment where project deadlines and targets were mounting. Karishma saw her immediate supervisor as a tough taskmaster, who at one point criticized her for a mistake she made in a presentation. For someone who was so reliant on external markers of achievement, hearing this feedback was difficult.

Following this incident, she would develop increasingly crippling self-doubt. She would question her position in life and doubt whether she even deserved being at such a prestigious post in this company. Thereafter, every presentation that she would deliver would be preceded by hours of looping thoughts: 'I don't deserve to be here' or 'I will make one mistake and that will be my unravelling' or 'before people discover my incompetence, it is better I quit myself.' These negative ruminations made it difficult for her to be at her best, and it became a self-fulfilling prophecy. After presentations, she would receive subpar feedback. And amid her sensitivity to feedback, a vicious cycle of ongoing doubt and rumination would ensue.

While the incident with her supervisor was a precipitating factor in this pattern of self-doubt, the seeds of this were sown in Karishma's childhood. The pressure of achieving developed into a sense that her self-worth was defined by her grades and exam results. The attitude that she imbibed was: 'You are only as good as your next exam result.' Also, Karishma wasn't particularly encouraged to acknowledge her part in her success. As a result, she withheld self-acceptance and self-compassion.

However, through therapy, Karishma learned how to identify this self-critical voice that had come to possess her. Identifying this voice requires some attention and practice, but it is something we all have the natural capacity to do.

Shachi Dalal, a Mumbai-based psychologist, says that the best way to handle this is to create a counter-voice that corrects the factual record. Karishma needed to list not just her negative assumptions but also her strengths and achievements thus far. Her strengths would include the very real virtues that had facilitated her success: hard work, diligence, intelligence, meticulousness, social skills and so on. Another step in this is to actively dialogue with the critical voice, rather than taking it at face value. Shachi Dalal suggested, 'Don't just accept the critical voice. Question it'.

The many people we look up to can make us feel like we will never live up to their standards. Life becomes miserable when we feel a constant need to prove ourselves to others. In the face of criticism, appropriate self-talk becomes crucial. It can make or break us. Over time, negative talk becomes a habit that leads to insecurity, hopelessness and shame.

Over time, Karishma would question the voice and counter it with evidence to establish her self-worth and her legitimate position in the company. She was able to identify unhelpful and unproductive thinking patterns, and ultimately abandon them for healthier ways of thinking. These skills helped Karishma to grow professionally and personally.

Ian Tuhovsky explains the various ways we create a toxic inner world. When we face routine difficulties, they feel like threats. The self-talk then distorts our perception of what has happened and treats it as a catastrophe. One is prone to imagine the worst, overanalyse and/or create a worst-case scenario. When one filters out the positives and accentuates the negatives, this creates fertile ground for engaging in harsh self-judgement, killing self-esteem.

Scott Mautz is a business inspirational speaker. He suggests following the '90 per cent rule' to cut the inner critic's influence. He explains that when you catch yourself engaging in negative self-talk, it should immediately trigger the reminder that 90 per cent of it will be unhelpful, misguided self-destruction, although 10 per cent might actually have something worth thinking about as a way to improve [6].

## RETHINK THE TALK

Our repeated thought patterns reinforce our beliefs, and our beliefs then define who we are and our actions which become our reality. Therefore, our automatic thoughts have a direct and immediate impact on our feelings or emotions, and on our behaviours [7].

There is an unreported epidemic of negative self-talk in our culture today, says Cynthia Kane, author of *Talk to Yourself Like a Buddhist*. She notes that many of us speak to ourselves in ways we would never speak to our worst enemy. The negative self-talk is when you beat yourself up or berate yourself for making a simple mistake, or when you compare yourself to others and feel that you are less important than they are. Everyone faces this dilemma. It stems from a world that has changed so rapidly, where expectations are set extremely high.

We live in a culture that expects us to be able to constantly do more with less time. We are plugged in and available 24/7 and tend to take on heavier workloads than ever before. This kind of competitive environment leads many to suffer from perfectionism. Psychologist and physical therapist, Dr Elizabeth Lombardo, author of *Better than Perfect*, says although some aspects of perfectionism can be positive—no one would argue that striving for excellence and being motivated to succeed are bad things—the problem with perfectionism is that it's an all-or-nothing mentality. 'It's either perfect or it's a failure and if it's a failure, then I'm a failure.'

When toxic self-judgement becomes self-hate, the torment can be worse than physical pain. Imagine living with someone who constantly badgers you with non-stop criticism and negativity. But it is not exactly another person—it is a nasty little voice in your head. If we are not attentive to its machinations, it can oppress our spirit non-stop.

The pain of self-judgement is compounded by the fact that it is invisible to others around us. When a person is suffering internally, few others can see the struggle or the pain. The troubled individual feels hollow inside but goes about their business, often outwardly projecting confidence. Many are so scared to try new things that they miss out on opportunities. Their fear of failure, of being judged harshly, of shame and embarrassment undermines their motivation.

We live in a world that is adept in the art of creating façades, where people share neatly packaged life narratives. Even if the outward displays are partially true, most successes involved untold episodes of mistakes, failures, shame and struggles, but typically little of that is shared. The rosy world that is outwardly projected makes us needlessly feel bad about our own lives. These feelings may weaken our drive to focus on our goals.

People are not perfect. Nobody breezes through their social and work life effortlessly. On the contrary, everyone experiences suffering. There is a constant bombardment of seemingly perfect images in advertisements and social media. These spaces are populated by carefully curated selfies and even air-brushed images, which can outstrip our sense of perspective. We tend not to share our true feelings of weakness, the behind-the-scenes strife and pain. The universal human vulnerability is a rich part of life, something that we as a society need to share.

## RETHINK PERFECTIONISM

Why do we let this voice get into our minds and affect us so deeply? One part of the answer is perfectionism. Perfectionists have surely been around for millennia, but systematic research on perfectionism has increased in recent decades. This research tells us that it has been linked to depression, anxiety disorders, anorexia, obsessive-compulsive disorder and insomnia [8].

Beth Leung, a 30-year-old Hong Kong-based lawyer, has always struggled with perfectionism in her professional and daily life. She studied in boarding school since the age of 16, and every holiday

## Chapter 4: Big Talk Small Talk

she would return home and she would dread her mother's critical eye. 'In the Asian community, the traditional family upbringing is quite different from the Western culture. My mother is a wonderful loving woman, but she tends to be very critical and eager to point out each apparent flaw she could spot in the name of giving 'constructive advice'. If I am fat or thin and even with how I dress. She has always been a perfectionist being the eldest in her family and having had a successful career before she had me and my brother. Often our relationship takes a strain as a result.'

With this see-sawing mother–daughter dynamic, Leung finds it difficult to engage with her mum. Her mother's supportive statements often belied a thinly veiled layer of judgementalism. When Leung went to boarding school in the UK, she gained a lot of weight due to homesickness and pressure from schoolwork. When she returned, her mother commented insensitively that she basically rolled out of the airport due to her comparatively chubby appearance since she last saw her daughter. Leung tried not to be affected by her comment, but the thought of being 'imperfect' started to slowly seep into her every waking thought. The Asian crazed image of frail bony girls also made Leung a target of body shaming by her local friends. 'In Hong Kong, my local friends embraced the skinny look, which they believed was the perfect image of beauty.' Despite the criticisms from her family and friends, Leung has continued to do the sports she loved such as swimming and rock climbing. But her mother would discourage her by claiming that these 'masculine sports' would give her manly shoulders and would talk her out of buying any clothes that would expose her shoulders. It was disheartening. Over time, Leung internalized these impossible standards.

In university, Leung worked hard and earned her law degree. When she returned to Hong Kong and started working in the legal field, she was riddled with self-doubt. She would constantly berate herself at the tiniest mistake. She would read into every sign that her work was not up to par and blow it up in her mind. She would do extra work and was very careful how she portrayed herself. She did what she was asked and handled herself professionally. However, even slight mistakes would be magnified into a huge stain in her mind. At times, when Leung felt that she overlooked a minor work-related matter, she would feel terrible about it and wished that she was more like a computer—able to do and remember everything perfectly.

After a while, this process of beating herself up, mentally, over every minor error began taking a toll on her. Leung took a step back and decided to stop attacking herself. She started looking at the big picture, to have an overview of her life and to pat herself on the back for all the rights rather than dwell on the wrongs. If something was on her mind, she would talk to her fiancé, brother or her friends. It helped to put things in perspective and redirected her thinking. It helped her learn from her mistakes and move on. She still struggles when the inner critic highlights her mistakes. 'It takes some focus and self-awareness to value myself as much as I value others. I can look at myself and know that I am only human, and we learn and grow from every mistake that we make. I am happy with what I have achieved so far in my life and I should be proud of myself.' Leung now has a better grip on affirming her own qualities and doesn't let the smallest things get to her. She understands now that no one can put you down but yourself, and you are the only one who can lift yourself up again and never look back.

Perfectionism is a broad personality style characterized by a hypercritical relationship with one's self, said Paul L. Hewitt, who co-authored *Perfectionism: A Relational Approach to Conceptualization, Assessment, and Treatment* [9]. Setting high standards and aiming for excellence can be positive, but perfectionism is dysfunctional, Hewitt said, because it is highlighted by a person's sense of self as permanently flawed or defective.

Setting goals and pursuing them is a good thing. However, perfectionism refers to setting goals that are almost impossible. It becomes stressful when you cannot reach these arbitrary imaginary standards. The anxiety and negativity that perfectionism brings with it can get overwhelming.

A study called 'Perfectionism Is Increasing Over Time' found that young people are more burdened than ever [10]. This is caused by a mix of excessively high personal standards. Failing to reach those standards results in intense self-criticism. In this hyper-reactive state, feelings of shame or guilt crop up, leading to more self-doubt and pressure to excel at everything.

It's harder to get things done when we have zero tolerance for mistakes. Rather than seeking perfectionism, imagine recognizing that mistakes are rarely terminal. Imagine accepting that we are bound to have flaws, and this is nothing to be ashamed of. On the contrary, mistakes offer an opportunity to self-correct and move ahead.

Before long, the inner critic expands its reach to denigrate everything that one values in life. The problem is compounded when the negative energy is amplified by the abuse in our environment. If we are not attentive, it can devolve into a never-ending loop in which we judge ourselves through the eyes of others. All of this can leave us questioning our very existence.

## WORTHY OF PRAISE

According to Diana Malerba, a certified confidence coach, the feeling that we are not good enough comes from our self-beliefs, that is, ideas about who we are, ideas that develop initially in our formative years [11]. These ideas affect how we feel about ourselves, feelings which in turn influence how we behave, respond and act in adulthood. These ideas are so ingrained in us, we don't even realize that they are there. Every thought that floats in our minds carries an effect.

More recently, research has shown that negative self-talk can affect us in our gut. Literally, we feel our 'stomach is in knots'. Being hard on ourselves drains our energy. The feelings of listlessness or lack of inspiration dominate the mind. There is no mood to do anything new. Sleep gets affected and in the daytime, we are unable to focus on any project. Because of the constant inner critic raising its voice, we end up living in fear, find it hard to connect and fill up with anxiety at the thought of any new challenge. It's like you are mentally shrinking away from the world, hiding in a corner.

'Twenty years from now you will be more disappointed by the things you did not do than by the ones you did do.' Think about this quote by Mark Twain. Being mindless about the negative self-talk can lead to regrets. If the conversations in your head are negative, then the chances are high that you will not be living your life to your full potential. We keep feeling unsure of taking risks in life. We avoid new opportunities or looking for challenges. We lose the battle with the inner critic telling us we cannot do it, or we will fail.

Twenty years from now there is a chance that you will be looking back with regret, wishing you had been courageous enough to take risks. Learning from our mistakes is how we get better. We need to get 'thick-skinned' about criticism whether it stems internally or externally.

The standards of precision set by individuals with low self-esteem are unreachable. The bar is set impossibly high. Even if the person achieves a set goal, the critical self-judgements result in self-doubt. Low self-esteem creates behaviours that include struggling in saying no and difficulty in creating healthy boundaries.

They fall prey to the assumption that everybody looks at them with a critical eye. They are anxious that soon they will be fired, rejected or even publicly humiliated. There is a huge difference between the false image they have of themselves and what others see of them. They live in internal conflict and worry about 'what did she or he really mean when they gave me a compliment?' We see people holding back and playing small, mainly because of the inner conversations going on in their mind, the negative self-talk.

Shad Helmstetter has studied the concept of self-talk for over 30 years and has written more than 20 books on it. The way this author explains it in the book *Negative Self-talk How to Change It*, the reason for failure is the repetition of a belief in failure. Negative self-talk is the repetition of a belief in failure. He notes that 77 per cent or more of the unconscious mental programmes in our mind are negative. Thousands of thoughts are controlled by the programmes or beliefs we have spent years storing in the subconscious. It can be difficult to get rid of negative thought processes which have been ingrained for years and buried deep. We don't rationalize or justify why we think these thoughts. The mind doesn't see this as false information and soon enough, the negative self-talk becomes a programmed habit.

However, he believes that because of the brain's plasticity, negative self-talk can be erased or replaced. There are three ways to change self-talk from negative to positive.

First, be mindful of your self-talk. Second, edit the script each time you say anything negative. Third, restate the words in positive form. Listen to positive self-talk, repeating the words and phrases. Like learning a new language, one can retrain oneself to focus on the positives rather than the negatives.

## GOING BEYOND YOURSELF

One of the reasons we are stuck in the cycle of low self-esteem is being overly focused on ourselves. Research indicates that we tend to focus on what we lack, which leads one in an ego-driven direction. Therefore, the best way to boost self-esteem is to forget about *you* temporarily and think about others. According to psychologists, Jennifer Crocker and Amy Canevello, 'Nothing makes you more proud of yourself than knowing that you are making a positive difference in the lives of other people' [12].

Marty Schmidt has been a humanities teacher at Hong Kong International School for over two decades. He teaches history, English and religion courses. He is also the author of the *Wisdom Way of Teaching: Educating for Social Conscience and Inner Awakening in the High School Classroom*. He points out that many of his high-achieving students struggle with the inner critic. Paradoxically, however, the baseline presumption he operates by as a teacher is that the solution in silencing the inner critic is not focusing more on yourself, but less. And the way his school supports this is through service experiences and projects outside school that are often transformative. There is something special about helping others in need. Participants feel better about the world and about themselves. There is little place for the inner critic when we experience closely the lives of those who have so much less.

## BOTTOM LINE

A classic book that has helped me immensely, not just in my writing life but also to tackle my self-talk, is *Bird by Bird: Some Instructions on Writing and Life* by Anne Lamott. Her sense of humour gives her anecdotes a vividness that one will never forget. Lamott suggests imagining that each of our interior complainers is a mouse. Isolate one mentally, pick it up by the tail and drop it in a jar. Repeat. 'Then put the lid on and watch all these mouse people clawing at the glass.' Imagine the jar has a volume control. Turn it all the way up for a moment, then right down. 'Leave it down and then get back to your shitty first draft.'

Imagery like that helps retain the lesson.

We need these reminders in our daily life to tackle the squeaky voices warning us of impending doom and hampering our self-worth.

Do not feel that you are alone in this search for a mute button on the negative self-talk. There are hundreds of thousands of people who have trouble with their inner critic, and there are many expert opinions, psychologists' research papers, life and career coaches advising us on how to handle the hostile nagging voice. Ultimately, we have to figure out what works for us. In all cases, awareness of this voice is important. Then, we try to understand the reasons behind the hostile talk.

It is natural to wish we could melt away the inner critic entirely from our lives. However, this would be like pining for a permanent state of peace and happiness, which is not easy to achieve in our complicated world. While the internal voice of doubt may be diminished, it cannot be completely eliminated. We can study its habits and gradually learn to interfere with its machinations by questioning its claims. Similar to the way a ship captain navigates difficult waters, we can become wiser and learn to move forward despite the self-doubts.

Very often, the inner critic shows up because we are trying out something new and challenging, something outside our comfort zone. The ostensible goal of the inner critic is safety. The precautionary thinking that drives the inner critic can protect us from unknowns, risks and embarrassments.

So there is no harm in embracing the inner critic with some gratitude, rather than stiffly resisting it. Suppressing or resisting the inner critic will not shut it up; it will only get louder. But we do want to recognize that this hyper protectiveness is unhealthy, and in the end, it holds us back. Facing it will help develop an understanding of how to manage it and give us insight into our choices. We can appreciate the warning signals because sometimes a warning is just what we need. But we face it knowing that we will nonetheless make the best choice and this inner critic does not have the final say.

## REFERENCES

1. The Economist. Japan's bullying bosses. The Economist; 2020. Available from: https://www.economist.com/business/2020/06/11/japans-bullying-bosses
2. Wignall N. 10 Types of negative self-talk (and how to correct them). NickWignall; 2018. Available from: https://nickwignall.com/negative-self-talk/
3. Hannaford J. Zoom interview. Hong Kong; 2020 July 7.
4. Bansal S, Schmidt M. Dealing with the accuser: befriending your inner critic. 2018. Available from: https://www.martinschmidtinasia.wordpress.com/2018/01/27/
5. Niiya Y, Brook AT, Crocker J. Contingent self-worth and self-handicapping: do contingent incremental theorists protect self-esteem? Self Identity. 2010; 9:276–297.
6. Mautz S. Following the '90 percent rule' will make you stop undermining yourself with negative self-talk. Inc. Com; 2019 May 6. Available from: https://www.inc.com/scott-mautz/following-90-percent-rule-will-make-you-stop-undermining-yourself-with-negative-self-talk.html
7. FutureLearn. Thoughts, feelings and behaviours. Future Learn; n.d. Available from: https://www.futurelearn.com/courses/depression-young-people/0/steps/36858

8. Rettner R. The dark side of perfectionism revealed. Live Science; 2010 July 11. Available from: https://www.livescience.com/6724-dark-side-perfectionism-revealed.html
9. Hewitt PL, Flett GL, Mikail SF. Perfectionism: a relational approach to conceptualization, assessment, and treatment. New York, NY: The Guilford Press; 2017.
10. Curran T, Hill AP. Perfectionism is increasing over time: a meta-analysis of birth cohort differences from 1989 to 2016. Psychol Bull 2019 April;145(4):410–429. Available from: http://dx.doi.org/10.1037/bul0000138
11. Malerba D. n.d. Available from: http://www.thebravehearted.ch/how-to-get-clear-on-self-confidence-or-self-esteem/
12. Crocker J, Canevello A. Social motivation: costs and benefits of selfishness and otherishness. Annu Rev Psychol 2017 January;68:299–325. Available from: https://ssrn.com/abstract=2896727; http://dx.doi.org/10.1146/annurev-psych-010416-044145

# CHAPTER 5

# TOXIC WORKPLACE

*It is not the strongest of the species that survive, nor the most intelligent, but the one most responsive to change.*

—Charles Darwin

## SET-UP TO FAIL

If a person starts to fail at their job and feels unhappy, how can they know if it's them or something about the workplace? Using 'toxic' to describe a workplace dates back to the late 1960s. In the 1980s, the meaning of 'toxic' expanded to include workplace behaviour and regulations. The word became popular after Virginia K. Baillie used it in her book, *Effective Nursing Leadership: A Practical Guide*, to shed light on the poor work environment nurses faced every day. She revealed the rules that dictated how nurses had to behave—to have the leadership skills of a man and the caring demeanour of a woman—and explained how harmful these dictates were. These requirements were so strict that they created unhealthy work environments, to say nothing of the sexism and discrimination [1].

We spend on average 8–10 hours a day at work, some even more. Our workplace and colleagues become as familiar to us as our home and family. In that sense, our self-worth is also inextricably tied to our workplace environment.

The first day at a new job may be among the most memorable moments of your career. The first office job almost always involves a learning curve, whether you are a fresh graduate entering the workforce or a seasoned professional person transitioning careers. Entering office life can be intimidating at first and you wouldn't be the first to experience culture shock.

'Most of us remember our first days at every job because of the heightened pressure to impress', says Lynn Taylor, a national workplace expert and author of *Tame Your Terrible Office Tyrant: How to Manage Childish Boss Behavior and Thrive in Your Job*. The natural urge to impress can take you off-track, so it is important to remember that you are already hired—you don't have to wow your new colleagues, Taylor says. It's every new employee's dream to be heralded for how brilliant and personable they are, or how they seem to 'get' the company so quickly. But that can cause a lot of wasted energy; you'll impress naturally, and more so once you understand the ropes [2].

Traditionally, the workplace has been a source of positive self-esteem because the employee has a meaningful role and because achievements bring about a natural boost of self-confidence. However, in our changing world, the modern workplace is marked by serious psychological stress factors, be it the demanding pace of work, the lack of acknowledgement, the punishingly long hours or the competition for productivity. These high pressures can create self-doubt about whether one is capable.

We know that competence is essential to workplace success, professional achievement and personal satisfaction. But without confidence, skill takes us only so far.

We try our best to bring out our best in the workplace, but what happens if our office has a negative environment. Every morning we dread going to work. No matter how hard we try to maintain healthy self-esteem, someone or some incident finds a way to crush it. For certain individuals, this happens every single day of their lives. Being saddled with a terrible supervisor can turn even the best job into a nightmare. Unfortunately, not every boss is the model of managerial perfection one would hope for. More people than not consider themselves stuck with a 'bad boss'.

'Mental health is the single most important health issue in the workplace. This is not only because mental health problems, including substance abuse, are a leading cause of lost productivity and sickness, but because workplace practices can worsen or enhance the mental health of workers', says Vikram Patel, professor and research fellow, Department of Global Health and Social Medicine, Harvard Medical School [3].

Dr Annie McKee is the author of *How to Be Happy at Work* and co-author of *Primal Leadership, Resonant Leadership* and *Becoming a Resonant Leader*. She suggests that for many professionals, fragile high self-esteem can paradoxically also be a by-product of success. People who excel at school and then in the workplace often get a tremendous amount of positive feedback—more, maybe, than they think they deserve. This affirmation doesn't last forever. Many employees experience the reality of bullying bosses, poisonous colleagues and soul-crushing cultures daily. 'Toxic organizations are rampant with conflict, fear and anger. The environment causes people to have physiological responses as if they're in a fight-or-flight situation. Healthy people become ill. Cold, flu and stress-related illnesses like heart attacks are more common. By contrast, in resonant organizations, people take fewer sick days and turnover is low. People smile, make jokes, talk openly and help one another.'

The corporate world is often characterized as VUCA, a world where volatility, uncertainty, complexity and ambiguity rule. For employees, managers and even the top brass who operate in such an atmosphere, stress can quickly turn into distress, anxiety and depression [4].

We've all worked with someone 'difficult', a co-worker known to say something wildly inappropriate or blow up. As it happens, the sense that 'the guy is mad' is often right: a fair number of impossible-to-get-along-with employees do have full-fledged personality disorders [5].

Eve Leung worked for eight years in a fashion apparels company. A devoted professional, she threw herself enthusiastically into her job as head of the product and design division. She ran it exceedingly well. Eve was professional and dedicated. She was a stellar manager of her creative team and formed great relationships with the clients and sales managers. The directors recognized her value. She was building the business for them and the company was doing well.

However, Eve had to deal with a thorny boss, Fiona Karmel, one of the founders of the company. The boss was a ruthless and cynical woman.

Fiona did not like Eve. At times, she would insult her in front of her team. Most of the product design ideas were criticized. She made Eve second guess her every decision. Fiona lorded over everyone with an air of cavalier superiority, making every day unbearable. For the final two to three years in her job, Eve struggled in the toxic work environment.

To undermine Eve, Fiona would take it upon herself to reassign one of her creative team members to another project. Eve would be left in the dark. In another incident, Fiona had an angry showdown with a subordinate, who would then not turn up for work. It disrupted the work environment and created distrust among the other team members as well. It made it hard to get basic things done. For Fiona, Eve was never good enough; Fiona would saunter in and say that Eve wasn't creative.

At times, it seemed like Fiona was actually acting out of jealousy because of the respect and recognition that Eve was receiving.

The emotional wear and tear was terrible and it was taking a toll on Eve.

After a while, Eve was assigned to a different board member to whom she reported to and during that time, Eve was able to perform better. She even set up a sustainable arm of the business, sourcing materials in a way that was more environment friendly.

But Fiona still wouldn't let it be. She continued to interfere and gripe endlessly. After a few months, Eve had had enough. There was a face-to-face conflict that got heated between Fiona and Eve. Ultimately, Eve knew that the situation had reached a stage where she would have to resign or she would be terminated. One day later, when Eve announced her decision, her team came into her office in tears.

Fiona, the toxic boss, sauntered in with three new people to replace Eve, whom she called her dream team. One of them got the creative director role, the position Eve had long hoped for. Fiona had the gall to celebrate with champagne and cakes in front of Eve. It was tasteless and insensitive. Eve was devastated by this disrespect after all the work she had put into the company. She decided that she would never give her heart to another person's business. She was filled with anger that the company which she had helped build had required that she sign a letter that she was resigning because she 'had to take care of her family'. It was demeaning. Nothing was based on merit or performance. On the contrary, every aspect of the company was marred by Fiona's egotism and jealousy. But Eve is determined to create her path. Using her industry knowledge, she plans to start her own business. 'If you got heart, you could make anything happen' [6].

In the case study of Eve and Fiona, the problem was not the company but the boss. Other research sheds light on this. A Danish study of 4,500 public service workers has provided credence to the adage that 'people don't leave jobs, they leave managers'. According to psychologist Matias Brødsgaard Grynderup, one of the researchers behind the study, 'We may have a tendency to associate depression and stress with work pressure and workload; however, our study shows that the workload actually has no effect on workplace depression' [7].

## OUTER EVENTS ALTER SELF-WORTH

We have known for some time that people are generally sensitive to the perception and evaluation that others, especially bosses, have about them. A person's feelings of self-worth are partially dependent on others' evaluation. We are highly motivated to seek others' approval, acceptance and affection, and avoid rejection. We manage our image to the extent we can, but research has found that the absence of approval can be a source of anxiety. Positive responses from others foster psychological and physical well-being, whereas long-term exposure to negative reactions is associated with psychological strain and poor physical health.

Externals are outer events or circumstances that can alter our self-worth. Like a dark shadow cast over us, we are pushed by authority to doubt ourselves. It comes in different forms. A difficult fact of life in many places is the ongoing presence of discrimination in the workplace. At times, employees are insulted and even abused due to colour, race, caste, creed, disability, gender or for just being in a disadvantaged position. Over time, feelings of being rejected and ostracized can lead to someone feeling shattered inside.

Poor self-esteem often leads to a fear of taking on new challenges and it can lead to unproductive work behaviours such as defensiveness or being overly compliant or rebellious. Low self-esteem is noticeable. In the workplace, this can prove to be a disadvantage. In the office environment, colleagues, bosses and even clients will take this as a negative attitude. There is a general belief that people with low self-esteem shy away from work, they are incompetent and lazy [8].

In the perfect world, everyone would possess unshakable self-esteem that is not dependent on comparison or competition with others. As adults, we should have developed intrinsic self-worth, ideally a kind of saintly equanimity that allows us to thrive independently of external influences. We must be sturdy and not blame the world for all our woes. However, the world is partly responsible. The long-term effects of a lifetime of rejection can kill one's inner spark and destroy the motivation to achieve success in life.

It may be difficult to believe that today in the 21st century, discrimination in the workplace is still a major issue, but as much as we would like to think that we live in a world full of compassion and tolerance, this just sadly isn't the case.

## INDIA'S CASTE SYSTEM

Some people are ostracized due to no fault of their own. They are just born into the wrong caste. Indian history is a story of wide-ranging and pervasive discrimination. In ancient India, the practice of untouchability, and the labelling of certain people as 'untouchables', was one of the most pernicious forms of discrimination. It remains a glaring reality even today. Caste is in a sense similar to a social class, but mobility is impossible and discrimination can occur even among those of the same economic class [9].

India's caste system was officially abolished in 1950, but the 2,000-year-old social hierarchy imposed on people by birth still exists in many areas of life. The caste system categorizes Hindus at birth, defining their place in society, what jobs they can do and who they can marry.

Like many migrants to America from India, Suraj Yengde is well-educated. At 30, he has a doctorate and a Master of Laws degree. Since 2016, he has been a graduate and postgraduate researcher at Harvard University.

He is from a small city, at least by Indian standards, where his father worked a series of menial jobs. Yengde was born into a family of 'untouchables', now more commonly known as Dalits. 'Caste is primarily an occupation-based system. You are given the position in the job hierarchy', he says. 'So the filthiest or the lowest-considered jobs were given to the "Untouchable" population, and their ancestors and their ancestors and on and on have been doing the same job—cleaning the human filth with their bare hands.'

Yengde's remarkable life trajectory illustrates the immense obstacles that Dalits face in India, and how he overcame those hurdles and arrived in the USA. Yengde, other Dalit activists and respondents to a 2018 survey say that, when surrounded by others of Indian descent, caste bias follows them like a shadow to what many have long regarded the land of the free—America [10].

Children don't naturally discriminate. It is internalized. As we age, we learn from our elders to judge, compare, criticize, worry and blame, obsess over faults, evaluate and fight. We are told from history, culture and society that it is okay to discriminate against others.

## CASTE DELUSION

A closer look at how the so-called members of the upper castes, for instance, a Brahmin, behave with the so-called members of the lower castes, for instance, a Dalit, is suggestive of the fact that they suffer from a kind of mental illness, which can be referred to as caste delusion.

In the field of psychiatry, a delusion is a false opinion or belief a person has developed which cannot be shaken by reason. The caste delusion, which is indeed the consequence of the caste system, has seriously impaired the mindset of both the upper castes and the lower castes. As a result, both have lost their capacity to see each other fully as human beings;

both have lost their capacity to recognize and respect each other based on their merit [11].

In earlier times, a person belonging to Brahmin caste, the upper caste, was conditioned to develop a phobia such that he/she feared to even see the lower-caste Dalit. With changing times, this may have improved, but there are a few segments which still harbour the same conservative belief.

And if a Brahmin happened to see a Dalit after setting out, he/she might actually return home and start his/her journey anew after bathing. The Dalit, for his/her part, was prone to feel guilty and developed a fear that he/she, for having 'violated' the Brahmin's space, will be cursed in retribution by the Brahmin, endangering his/her life and property and that of his/her relatives.

A Dalit who accepts his lot and doesn't aspire to higher education or a better life comes to internalize his/her status as untouchable. For such a person, low self-worth and low self-esteem are only natural. The birth-ascribed low social status also leads to identity confusion, self-hate, hypertension, neuroticism and perception of the world as a hostile place [12].

India has taken steps to eliminate the caste system. Untouchability is outlawed and the caste system is not practised as it once was, not at least in bigger cities. However, the centuries-old thinking is deeply ingrained. Like the injustices towards Africans and Americans, the echo of past discriminatory structures tends to persist despite legislative efforts. Thus, the isolation and segregation of untouchables in India continue.

As professional mobility increases, the emergence of the 'educated among the deprived' has created a new workplace environment. Individuals from traditional tarnished occupations are moving in greater numbers into white-collared office jobs. Employees, including individuals from the so-called lower castes, are exposed to various psychological vulnerabilities and mental health strain.

Environments associated with social rejection immediately elicit negative emotions such as sadness, loneliness, hurt, anger, jealousy and lower self-esteem in the victims. Socially rejected individuals typically find themselves withdrawing from interpersonal interactions. Individuals may isolate themselves physically to avoid contact with a psychologically threatening environment. It becomes a habit to expect hostility and to be on guard. Even those who occupy the same physical space may nonetheless isolate socially and psychologically.

Dr Tarunabh Khaitan, a law professor at Oxford University suggests, '…almost everyone in India has been a victim of some sort of discrimination, and almost everyone has also been a perpetrator' [13].

## GENDER BIAS IN THE WORKPLACE

For centuries, women have faced discrimination at home and workplace. Melinda Gates has become a leading light on this issue, committing herself to expand women's power and influence in the USA. By pledging one billion dollars over the next decades, she hopes to shake up the system. In her view, the absence of women in positions of power and influence for most of the history seems to be the norm. Equality cannot wait, she says [14].

A recent United Nations report has conveyed that despite decades of progress, closing the equality gap between men and women is a gradual process. Close to 90 per cent of men and women hold some sort of bias against women, suggesting invisible barriers women face in achieving equality. According to the report, about half of the world's men and women feel that men make better political leaders and over 40 per cent feel that men make better business executives and that men have more right to a job when jobs are scarce [15].

Self-esteem plays a significant role in how men and women view themselves in the workplace. This is important because self-perceptions can trigger different ways of relating to work. While more women now work in traditionally male-dominant environments such as technology, transportation, mining, police forces, manufacturing and construction, research shows that differences persist in the way women and men feel about their roles.

For instance, studies show that women more frequently express feeling that they don't deserve their job or merit associated with their title. They tend to worry more about being disliked and about not being as smart as others in their fields. Although men doubt themselves too, they are less likely to allow their doubts to interfere with their goals. Studies show that women tend to apply for jobs if they are 90 per cent sure that it matches with their skills, whereas men will apply if the role matches their abilities by only 20 per cent [16].

Cathy Guisewite is the creator of the *Cathy* comic strip and recently the author of *Fifty Things That Aren't My Fault: Essays from the Grown-up Years*. The book, a collection of observations about aging, is her first book of essays and her first major project since ending *Cathy*. Guisewite remembers well the first day the comic strip ran on 22 November 1976; she hid in the bathroom at work for most of it. She was 26 years old and working at an advertising agency in Detroit as a copywriter, and she was terrified that she would be laughed off at the office if anyone saw the strip. For one thing, she didn't know how to draw, and she fretted that the artists in her office would pick apart her crude illustrations. But she also worried that her colleagues would see her as weak. 'I had worked so hard to develop myself as a professional person', she said, 'and this comic strip was coming out about my most vulnerable moments'. She was concerned they would never see her again without thinking of her cartoonish avatar, a lonesome woman waiting for a man to call.

This depiction of (mostly middle-class, mostly White) femininity may have been melodramatic, but it was a candid depiction of Guisewite's preoccupations: Will I ever get married? Have children? Meet my mother's impossible standards? Feel good in a swimsuit? In committing these nagging questions to the page, Guisewite developed a loyal fan base. *Cathy* was intentionally hyperbolic, almost a parody of its time. Those were the transitional years of American feminism. Women were entering the workforce in power suits but hadn't quite reconciled how that decision might destabilize every other aspect of their lives. It was not always clear how to balance that external liberation with their interior lives. They delayed marriage or child rearing while they climbed the career ladder. They craved romantic partnerships but struggled not to be viewed sexually in the workplace. *Cathy*, Guisewite said, was her way of processing what it felt like to be sandwiched into an impossible generation [17].

Guisewite uses the term sandwich generation to refer to the tendency for some women to be everything to everyone, the I-am-responsible-for-everyone's-well-being reality. Many women stretch themselves to be perfect at the workplace and the home. It doesn't always work out well. The problem with people pleasing is that instead of taking responsibility for building self-worth, our self-worth is defined by others' responses.

People pleasing, which typically involves not asserting yourself, is an issue widespread in most companies. Saying 'no' or setting boundaries in a professional context can prove to be difficult for some of us. It may be motivated by a desire to impress others at work or by the fear of being negatively judged by a boss or colleague. The people-pleasing syndrome can have serious consequences on those who are afflicted. The good news is that you can learn at any age how to respect your needs and desires. Being assertive doesn't mean stepping on other peoples' toes or becoming selfish, but merely being direct about conditions that are unacceptable to you.

But there are trailblazing women in many male-dominated industries, women who are asserting themselves and proving their capabilities. Kim Se-yeon was born in the South Korean city of Daejeon. She started playing video games when she was just five years old. Today, she plays for the Shanghai Dragons in the Overwatch League, a professional e-sports league produced by Blizzard Development. Se-yeon is better known by her gamer nickname Geguri. Geguri played the character Zarya, a powerful tank that can absorb incoming blows and redirect them towards her opponents in the form of a laser beam, and she found that she was extremely good at her aiming techniques. She possessed such great skill in this that her community found it unbelievable, so much so that she was accused of using an automatic aiming software—cheating. Being guilty of such a violation can get a pro-player permanently expelled from the league. But after she proved her talent in a monitored studio, her name was cleared. Geguri was taken aback by the people who accused her, but this opportunity to prove her skill won her a lot of support. As the only female player in the league, she feels the pressure to inspire many other women who look up to her and hope to achieve her position some day [18].

Why do we discriminate?

Gordon Allport is a psychologist who believes that discriminating against others is part of our natural way of thinking. In his book *The Nature of Prejudice*, he explains that grouping is a form of presumptions we make about people. 'We cannot possibly avoid this process. Orderly living depends upon it.'

We make sense of our world by categorizing information into groups. This form of thinking enables us to interrelate or react quickly, but it can also lead to wrong presumptions. We commit mental errors that result from our tendency to quickly bundle information and label them. Research suggests that prejudice comes from a deep psychological process in which discomfort with ambiguity makes people prone to make generalizations about others [19].

## QUIT BEING A PUSHOVER: BE ASSERTIVE

Cecilia Cheung has worked for a multinational corporation for over a decade. She shares her experience working in a corporate culture. This was the time when no one spoke openly about discrimination or gender bias. There's much wisdom in her journey [20].

After Cheung joined the company, within five months, she got a promotion. After that, for the next few years, she received great performance reviews but no further promotion. 'My boss shared some constructive criticism. It was balanced and measured overall. Despite getting the glowing reviews, getting that second promotion took a long time.'

For the next five years, Cheung noticed that her other colleagues were being promoted from manager to senior manager. 'It was surprising that I wasn't receiving the same advantages. I was responsible for Asia, working out of the Hong Kong office in a regional role. My American and European counterparts were getting into senior managerial positions, while I was running the whole department within Asia.'

Cheung said that her male colleagues in Europe were being promoted quickly despite the fact that they were doing less work and had less responsibility. She was working hard and proving her worth in the company. However, she had a tough time getting what she deserved. 'If I look objectively at my scope of work, I had taken on a great responsibility and there were people reporting to me.'

Cheung's response to this situation was to do more. 'That's the immigrant in me. I always thought that the way to deal with this bias was to work harder and harder. I was born in Hong Kong and I moved to Canada when I was eight. My parents had the very typical kind of immigrant parent mentality. Especially if you're Chinese, I always had in the back of my head, my father saying: "you're always going to have to work twice as hard." I'm going to have to be exceptional. I'm going to have to be so undeniably good and be better than others to achieve the same as other people. This thought process was instilled in me. I struggled with that because I thought I knew internally that I was doing as good, if not a better job as anybody. It was the myth of exceptionalism. I had to be exceptional and I had to be twice as good to get half of that. I was so stuck in this self-sabotaging mindset that I started judging myself about not being perfect. Is there some fault of mine, some ability-based fault that actually I'm not good enough? And I think that's where the self-esteem part is especially interesting.'

Cheung reflects on the past. 'In a way, it's easy for me now at the age of 45, having gone through that throughout my 30s and being able to look back with hindsight and understand what that situation was. My boss was saying that I was doing a good job. I began to wonder if there was something systemically wrong with this company or was it because there was something wrong with what I was doing.'

Her self-doubt increased when she noticed that although her performance reviews were great, there would typically be some weakness that needed improvement. She would feel that she wasn't getting her promotion or salary bump because of that weakness. It became an issue of self-esteem. 'I think it was the lack of self-esteem that I didn't ask for the raise. I should have just asked even if they said no. I should have still asked for it.'

Those were tough few years for her. She soon realized that it wasn't just about working harder and being better. She had to address this issue of being denied her promotion and salary bump.

'I had those five years where I did not negotiate and yes, I was paid well, but for the value of my position it wasn't balanced. In hindsight, in the early part of my career when I didn't speak up, I left a lot of money on the table. It was in the last four or five years that I was paid better. I was expatriated, worked in Europe and got all those benefits. That was what gave me the nest money to start my business.'

Cheung's advice is to be upfront. 'Don't leave all that money on the table. It's not about being greedy. It's about your value. If you do a good job and the salary is not within that range, then ask for it. It is a capitalist system. There's a supply and a demand. So if you've handled your position and job well, that becomes money, which gives you all the freedom and the ability to go and chase after the things that you dreamed to do.' Her advice to young people is that you may think it is okay to not ask your due. 'If you think you don't deserve that extra 5 per cent bump to your salary, you ask yourself what difference will 5 per cent make.'

However, over a lifetime, it does make a difference.

Cheung added that in the past couple of years, those around her were increasingly talking about diversity and inclusion (D&I). 'Around 2013–2014, while I was at the headquarters of my company working in its design department, the CEO of the company talked about the importance of D&I. Efforts were made to set up programmes and the key executives were tasked to take up D&I topics that needed to be addressed.'

Cheung noted that most corporate environments in the last decade have come to address the related equity issue of the glass ceiling as well.

'In the span of my career, my manager gave me great opportunities, and ultimately did give me three promotions. Through the course of eight or nine years, he enabled me to travel the world for my job, put me through all kinds of training, and offered mentoring and performance sessions. I owe a lot to that person, but he was the same person who held me back in my promotion for three years in a row and who wasn't always open and honest with me about some situations.'

Ultimately, it seemed clear that he was prejudiced. 'My manager believed, probably much more, in promoting the White people than people of colour. He believed more in promoting men than women. And as a woman of colour, I was doubly disadvantaged.'

She says that in light of her experience, it is important that young people in new jobs understand these office dynamics. Office culture can affect morale. Sometimes promotions are not based on merit. 'Often it is not about the self-esteem you bring to work, but that work literally starts eating away your self-esteem.'

Cheung's friend, Rebecca Lai, had a horrible boss who made ridiculous demands on her. And when she tried to stand up for herself, he gaslighted her and she ended up feeling that she wasn't good enough. For three to four years in her new job, even though it was a very healthy environment, she still doubts herself. The leftover feelings of self-doubt linger. Even though a decade has passed since that first job, she still winces at the thought of it.

Cheung offers some useful advice. 'I wish in my 30s, I had the benefit of not only a mentor, but other women who I could talk to and share in depth about a work environment or to ask the questions, how do I negotiate a higher salary? How do I negotiate a promotion?'

After a few years, she gained confidence to negotiate. 'It was no longer a self-esteem discussion. It was simply, this is how the systems work. This is the role that we discussed. This is what I deserve. It was not about my self-esteem, it was not making it out about me, but about my merit and performance.'

Cheung looks back at her corporate experience and feels that she got a lot out of it because she was skilled at her job and confident to the point where she was able to negotiate.

She said that a person who is very young in their career needs to arm themselves with the ability to look at a situation and understand it objectively. If they feel overwhelmed and are unable to express themselves, it becomes harder to cope. For example, if there is a toxic person on the team or any other issue that is biased, talk about it, tell the manager. If nothing is done to change the situation, then it is a toxic culture. They are upholding that culture in a way. Take responsibility for yourself and move to another company.

Young people starting out in their career often benefit from having mentors to guide them. Search your network for individuals who can offer this sort of advice on career and workplace issues. Recruiters may also serve as mentors. The main thing is to know your interests and stand up for yourself.

## DISCRIMINATION AND MENTAL HEALTH

Years of research indicate that people are deeply affected by discrimination. The effect ranges from self-esteem issues to stress-related disorders, anxiety and depression, explains Vickie Mays, who is a health policy and management professor at UCLA Fielding School of Public Health [21]. It is often the case that when a person suffers from low self-esteem for a long period of time, they cope with the stress through unhealthy habits. This could be alcoholism and smoking.

In another USA-based study done in 2007, Asian Americans who had experienced discrimination were more likely to develop mental health issues which would ultimately need treatment. Gilbert Gee, a professor at the Fielding School's Department of Community Health Sciences, instigated this study. 'Much of the research has focused on symptoms of sadness and anxiety resulting from the mistreatment, and that's very important, but we wanted to look at clinical outcomes', Gee says. He discovered a clear correlation between discrimination and the likelihood of mental disorders [22].

Discrimination has various aspects and is experienced differently. Researchers are not sure about the process by which it affects mental health. 'There are so many different routes, some of them direct and some of them indirect', Gee explains. He also added that friends and relatives of the victim of discrimination are affected too by the constant negativity in their community.

There are direct and indirect ways that indicate discrimination. Some are openly insulted due to their race, colour, gender and other factors. Others may be rejected from a job or declined service at a restaurant or not allowed residence in a certain apartment building. This author has faced discrimination where a taxi driver did not stop when hailed, but just a short distance away stopped for a person from a Western background. These are small incidents, but over time can affect a person's mindset. Researchers have shown that these kinds of experiences affect us, make it harder to function in our daily lives.

For many people, coming to terms with who they are and forming a positive sense of identity can be complicated. This occurs when they are seen as different from those around them, or if they feel like the odd one out.

## INCLUSION: EVERYONE MATTERS

The population of young people who identify as LGBTQ+ is growing. For individuals who identify as LGBT (lesbian, gay, bisexual, transgender) or are questioning this facet of their personality, establishing a positive sense of self can sometimes be difficult. Some LGBTQ+ people are embracing their sexual or gender identities, as they have many supportive people around them who understand and appreciate them for exactly who they are. It is unfortunately common that LGBTQ+ people struggle with developing a positive sense of self.

Being gay or transsexual is not a choice, and it's not something a person can 'catch' or become due to influences around them. If this were the case, then people who were raised and educated purely by heterosexual and non-trans people would not be LGBTQ+, which is not what we observe. People can often feel pressured to conform to society's conventional ideas of being male or female. Those who do not fit the category can be subjected to ridicule, intimidation and even physical abuse.

Even though there is an increasing acceptance of LGBTQ+ people in society and greater visibility in the media and public life, many LGBTQ+ people still experience discrimination, harassment and violence at work, school and in social situations. Individuals subject to such discrimination may experience a greater prevalence of mental health problems [23].

Can you be fired for being gay? Can you be jailed for it? Or lashed for it? Or can you prosecute someone for making a homophobic slur or treating you like a second-class citizen? The answers to these questions depend entirely on the country you live in—and the laws that have been put in place by the government of each state to either help or hinder the LGBTQ+ community.

Asia has both some of the harshest and most progressive LGBTQ+ laws in the world. To protect their citizens, local groups are trying to turn the former into the latter.

A landmark judgement was announced in September 2018 in India. The Chief Justice Dipak Misra, in recognition of the LGBTQ+ community, said, 'I am what I am so take me as I am'. The Supreme Court struck down a 157-year-old law, Section 377, of the Indian Penal Code. This was an outdated legacy of the British colonization in India; Section 377 rendered all sexual activities 'against the law of nature' punishable by law [24].

This outcome was the result of a long-term campaign by two female public interest litigators, Arundhati Katju and Menaka Guruswamy [25]. These change agents became beacons of hope for the LGBTQ+ community. 'We have to bid adieu to prejudices and empower all citizens', said the Chief Justice of India's Supreme Court. It was a powerful moment, and while local culture still needs to catch up, legalizing same-sex activity allows pressure groups to be far more vocal about advocating for equal rights in the workplace and education system. Indian companies are increasingly taking steps to make the workplace more diverse and inclusive, but much of these activities are only about recruiting more women for supporting, and not leadership, roles.

Asia, in general, lags behind Europe, North America and even parts of Africa when it comes to progressive LGBTQ+ laws. Taiwan legalized gay marriage and parliaments in countries including Japan, China and South Korea have begun looking into the process. Hong Kong courts are slowly relaxing same-sex marriage benefits through the courts and Thailand has a plan to legalize same-sex civil partnerships [26].

Many in our society remain ignorant to the hurt they are causing to their LGBTQ+ friends and family members. It is this ignorance that needs to be addressed.

Discrimination happens every day, in homes, in schools and workplaces.

## BOTTOM LINE

Everyone aspires towards something beyond what they are given or born into. In the rough-and-tumble of society, we are judged and, at times, unfairly. As a result, we continue on this cycle of proving our worth to others while validating our worth to ourselves. This interwoven relationship creates a gap between our core worth and how we are perceived by the outside world. It is like the spokes of a wheel, the centre being our inner truth and the various aspects (spokes) we display to the world enable us to keep the wheel turning towards our goal. To be able to 'fit in' or 'to be accepted', we suppress our own truth, hide our true nature. These complications undermine our ultimate search for happiness and meaning in life.

Our intrinsic self-worth is maintained through appropriate self-care. To a great degree, our inner mindset is in our control. Therefore, how we think, what choices we make and our behaviour are in our hands. But the environment is also important. Our workplace affects how we feel about ourselves.

## REFERENCES

1. Stojanovic M. Toxic work environment: how to recognize the red flags and what to do. Clockify; n.d. Available from: https://clockify.me/blog/business/toxic-work-environment/

2. Smith J. 19 things you should do on your first day of work. Business Insider; 2018. Available from: https://www.businessinsider.com/what-to-do-your-first-day-of-work-2018-3

3. Moses NV. Bosses must take care of employee mental health. Mint; 2018 September 6. Available from: https://www.livemint.com/Leisure/bKUyBCjfJmdk0ZcQ1ReiCM/Bosses-must-take-care-of-employee-mental-health.html

4. Nair D. One out of every two employees in corporate India suffers from anxiety and depression. YourStory.Com; 2016 September 24. Available from: https://yourstory.com/2016/09/depression-corporate-india

5. Banaji V. Corporate India's mental health crisis. People Matters; 2020 January 15. https://www.peoplematters.

in/article/technology/corporate-indias-mental-health-crisis-24337

6. Leung E. Phone interview. Hong Kong; 2020 August 20.

7. Warrell M. How to handle a bad boss: 7 strategies for 'managing up. Forbes; 2014. Available from: https://www.forbes.com/sites/margiewarrell/2014/01/20/6-strategies-to-hanhandldling-a-bad-boss/?sh=15d4ed226ea0

8. Alton L. Why low self-esteem may be hurting you at work. NBC News; 2018. Available from: https://www.nbcnews.com/know-your-value/feature/why-low-self-esteem-may-be-hurting-you-work-ncna829461

9. Singla T. Why #BlackLivesMatter is relevant to India: common history of discrimination. Eleventh Column; 2020 June 18. Available from: https://www.eleventhcolumn.com/2020/06/18/why-blacklivesmatter-is-relevant-to-india-common-history-of-discrimination/

10. Martin P. Suraj's shadow: wherever he goes, his caste follows—even in America. Pulitzer Center; 2019 February 25. Available from: https://pulitzercenter.org/reporting/surajs-shadow-wherever-he-goes-his-caste-follows-even-america

11. Jiloha RC. Deprivation, discrimination, human rights violation, and mental health of the deprived. Indian J Psychiatry. 2010;52(3):207–212. Available from: https://doi.org/10.4103/0019-5545.70972

12. Bhatnagar RC. India: caste, prejudice and the individual [Book review]. India Q. 1970 July;26(3):300–300. Available from: https://doi.org/10.1177/097492847002600335

13. NH Political Bureau. In India 'right to discriminate' seen as a 'private entitlement'. National Herald; 2017

March 17. Available from: https://www.nationalherald india.com/news/interview-a-comprehensive-anti-discrimination-law-is-long-overdue-in-india-says-dr-tarunabh-khaitan

14. Gates M. Melinda Gates: Here's why I'm committing $1 billion to promote gender equality. Time; 2019 October 2. Available from: https://time.com/5690596/melinda-gates-empowering-women/

15. Almost 90% of men/women globally are biased against women. UNDP; n.d. Available from: http://hdr.undp.org/en/content/almost-90-menwomen-globally-are-biased-against-women

16. Gino F, Wilmuth CA, Brooks AW. Compared to men, women view professional advancement as equally attainable, but less desirable. Proc Natl Acad Sci 2015;112(40):12354–12359. Available from https://doi.org/10.1073/pnas.1502567112

17. Schrobsdorff S. What happens when a woman has to be everything to everyone. Time; 2019. Available from: https://time.com/5560221/cathy-comic-creator-memoir-book-review/

18. Fitzpatrick A. Meet the female gamer taking the male-dominated world of esports by storm. TIME; 2019 May 16. Available from: https://time.com/collection-post/5584909/kim-geguri-se-yeon-next-generation-leaders/

19. Association for Psychological Science. Research states that prejudice comes from a basic human need and way of thinking. Association for Psychological Science; 2011. Available from: https://www.psychologicalscience.org/news/releases/research-states-that-prejudice-comes-from-a-basic-human-need-and-way-of-thinking.html

20. Cheung C. Zoom interview. Hong Kong; 2020 August 5.
21. Gordon D. Discrimination can be harmful to your mental health. UCLA; 2016. Available from: https://newsroom.ucla.edu/stories/discrimination-can-be-harmful-to-your-mental-health
22. UCLA. Discrimination can be harmful to your mental health. UCLA; 2016. Available from: https://www.uclahealth.org/discrimination-can-be-harmful-to-your-mental-health
23. Wandrekar JR, Nigudkar AS. What do we know about LGBTQIA+ mental health in India? A review of research from 2009 to 2019. J Psychosexual Health. 2020; 2(1):26–36.
24. Thomas M. 'Not an aberration but a variation': Indian Supreme Court judges on homosexuality. Quartz India; 2018. https://qz.com/india/1330419/section-377-indian-supreme-court-judges-remarks-on-lgbtq/
25. Chopra P. Arundhati Katju, Menaka Guruswamy are on the 2019 TIME 100. Time; 2019. Available from: https://time.com/collection/100-most-influential-people-2019/5567711/arundhati-katju-menaka-guruswamy/
26. Twigg M. Why laws in Asia need to catch up with the LGBTQ movement. GenT; 2019 July 17. Available from: https://generationt.asia/ideas/asian-law-lgbt-movement

## CHAPTER 6

# SOCIAL MEDIA TRAP

*It's healthy for your self-esteem to need less internet praise.*

—Taylor Swift

### PRE-SOCIAL MEDIA

If you grew up in the 1980s, you know what it felt like to be immersed in the real world, rather than at a screen. They have experienced their surroundings in a deeper, more sensory way, interacting real-time with real-life friends. Meals were shared without the distraction of a smartphone or the pressure to respond immediately to the electronic mode of communication. Music wasn't streamed nor was a book on a tablet. Life offered a different kind of peace.

But today, information overload is pervasive, and people are hyper-connected to every mode of contact. We cannot get through the day without responding or reacting to our smart devices. It has become an extension of our physical bodies. We are so immersed in gadgets that they affect our emotional well-being. We become vulnerable if we do not manage our internet use. Whether we use social media as a tool or as a means to maintain connectivity, we are at its mercy.

Studies have shown that social media feeds and posts have a direct impact on our self-esteem. We are under its spell when we find ourselves scrolling through hundreds of updates and posts. It covers, and is not limited to, even finding ourselves genuinely concerned with the likes and reactions of others. We too easily forget that our electronic habits are something we control. If it affects us, it is because we allow it.

But before we get into the adverse effects of social media, or how devalued we feel because of it, let us dwell a little longer on the time when this medium did not exist.

Those born in the 1960s can recall a much different way of life. Our thoughts, our choices and many of our decisions were based on our immediate surroundings. Access to information was limited. The way we communicated, in many countries, was defined by social tradition. Through our families, relationships and seniors, strong cultural values about modesty and self-effacement were instilled in us from a very young age. We learned to focus on work, not rewards. We were taught to be modest and humble in every area of our lives. Those who craved the limelight were not admired. We dealt with our challenges and weaknesses privately and quietly, rather than sharing them publicly. The way we were raised in the past was quite different from what we are experiencing now.

With the advent of social media, we are somehow expected to be more visible. Being open about one's views, ideas, life events and achievements is the norm. In our hi-tech era, our electronic public image shows that we are plugged into trends, and this enables us to stay abreast of the fast-changing environment.

Dr Jean Twenge, professor of psychology at San Diego State University, notes that the biggest difference between

Gen Y or Millennials, on the one hand, and their predecessors in Gen X (born between 1965 and 1980) is their way of seeing the world. The experiences that they have every day are fundamentally different.

Around 2012 and 2013, smartphones became widespread among school-aged students. 'It's also around the time that social media use among high school students started to become popular. The smartphone went from being introduced, to half the people having it in five years. It's the fastest adoption of technology as far as we can tell,' she notes [1].

The information we imbibe comes from streaming through the internet, colouring how we think and even what we perceive. Our immediate surroundings do not have the same effect as the social media dimension. Despite warnings issued by researchers worldwide of its negative effects, we remain wired almost continuously. It is a fundamental part of our lives. It has become almost impossible to live without social media.

Why is social media so important in our lives? Simple. Because almost everyone is on it. Unlike television, there are no gatekeepers on social media; everyone is a content creator. As a result, there is pressure to join social networking sites just to stay in the loop. Whether it is education, business, politics, social or climate awareness, everyone has a personal connection to the internet. Not only the young, but people of all ages and professions use social networking sites to receive information. People from all over the world share and influence opinions, create impressions, discuss political views and update pictures. Many spread fake news as well. The internet has made the world a smaller place by putting diverse nations, traditions, cultures and human behaviours on our screen. From that aspect, we are deeply influenced by what's happening outside our sphere, thousands of kilometres away. Imagine how much of an impact a stranger's post can have on our thoughts, beliefs and behaviour. Now imagine that a hundredfold.

## SOCIAL MEDIA COMPARISONS

According to Sanam Devidasani, a Mumbai-based counselling psychologist, 'Well-being is achieved when the gap between one's ideal self and real self is not too large. Social media is giving more room to increase that gap. To a great extent, this gap is determined by our own presence on social media and by the presence of others.'

This gap has increased exponentially. We have the power to present ourselves in any way we want. Many people put up a wall of illusions. Behind the digital curtain, we hide our weaknesses and flaws, our mistakes and failures, and project only that which will win us accolades.

Devidasani further explained that when we post on social media, we post happy moments of our lives. We appear too at our best, sharing our interesting and fun activities. She says:

> Even though we look our best, we still tend to put several filters, distort our bodies to look a certain way which is perceivably acceptable. This is not a representation of what our lives actually are. So we are essentially portraying ourselves as someone else. That unrealistic portrayal becomes our ideal self. This ideal self is moulded by what we think others will find attractive and also by what information we take online. The goals of our life are influenced by what we see online. To match up to what we see in other's posts, we up the ante when it comes to our portrayal, often forgetting that we are not posting as our real selves. This leads to immense pressure on ourselves to forever try to achieve

that unrealistic reality that we have made visible to others, leaving us utterly dejected and dissatisfied with our lives.

The 24/7 ease to share the 'perfect everything' robs us of opportunities to experience real life. We want to show you the best. As a result, pressure builds up to behave artificially in order to maintain a fake life that we claim to be living. This creates a domino effect when those who view our posts compare themselves negatively, believing that their lives have much to be desired. We feel that everyone else's life looks so easy [2].

In 2018, Instagram celebrated the milestone of reaching more than 1 billion users. The social media giant enables people to post images about their lives, whether in the kitchen or on a mountaintop, and the images can be easily altered. However, there is a catch: recent studies show that the ability to edit photos to perfection has spread insecurity in many people. 'The Instagram app that people use to document their life turned into one that determines how they live it.'

Despite these trends, nearly 80 per cent of teenagers were on Instagram, and nearly half of those users have been bullied on the platform. Studies have shown that online usage led to self-destructive behaviour. Sheri Bauman, a counselling professor at the University of Arizona, calls Instagram a 'one-stop-shop for the bully'. The company has done extensive research to develop artificial intelligence to root out insults, shaming and disrespect. Instagram's Head Adam Mosseri says, 'Technology isn't inherently good or bad in the first place. It just is. And social media, as a type of technology, is often an amplifier. It's on us to make sure we're amplifying the good and not amplifying the bad' [3].

Avinash Sujanani graduated with a Bachelor of Science degree in Economics, Finance and International Business. He says that after he returned to Hong Kong, Instagram did take a toll on him, but he says, 'It depends on who you are following and what you are viewing. I used to scroll through Instagram when I was bored at home. My friends and influencers would post pictures doing fun and cool things. This made me feel terrible about the fact that I was home and bored. The recurrence of this feeling grows and affects mental health and self-esteem. Therefore, I decided to take a social media detox and deleted Instagram for 4 months. I felt much better. When I downloaded the app again, my reason had changed, and I was a lot more in control. I now allow myself five minutes, a daily limit on my Instagram usage' [4].

Twenge recommends limiting leisure smartphone use to less than 2 hours per day, not including the time needed for professional work, homework and navigation. 'Smartphones are awesome; they do a lot of things for us. But they have to be a tool that we use and not a tool that uses us,' she concluded.

Devidasani too believes that 'Moderation is key. If the usage is excessive, it could lead to dependency which is not healthy for one's self-esteem. If used in moderation, even the "likes" and comments received on social media can be good for building one's self-esteem. Validation is something that everyone needs which is completely normal.'

'At times, if we were not given that validation from our parental figures when we were children, the need can persist through to adolescence and seep into adulthood', says Devidasani. People who continue to require constant validation during adulthood are more dependent on social media to gain it.

'What's problematic about this is that sometimes you may be met with invalidation. You are essentially leaving your self-esteem in the hands of others. If that's the case, that means that your self-worth is not determined by you but by others, most of whom are strangers.'

Real life loses its richness in the electronic world of artificially constructed images. Constant notifications to attend to the curated lives of others become addictive. It is a never-ending loop of inner turbulence, leading to self-esteem abuse, increased anxiety and restlessness.

## CREATING IMPRESSIONS: WORK

In general, we form preconceived notions of other people on the basis of what we observe on the surface. The admonition to not judge a book by its cover is a wise advice, but in reality it's difficult to do so. We are quick to judge people by how they appear to be.

We have all heard of the term 'elevator speech', a short and crisp overview of yourself on your strengths. Social media can be thought of as our unofficial elevator speech. A glance through someone's social page creates a distinct impression that can lead to comparisons, presumptions and positive or negative reactions.

It is not just what you share, but how much you share on social media that reflects on you positively or negatively. You have the power to create an image of yourself. Everything about you can be found online, and it's generally there forever. So even if you want to forget an embarrassing incident, Facebook will not let you forget. People read these posts and they judge. Even an innocent update can lead to misleading perceptions. It takes just one wrong picture or a post to create a bad impression.

Someone cleverly shared online: Just like you wouldn't drink and drive, don't drink and post, it can lead to disaster.

If you are looking for a job or aspiring to change your career, then what you share on social media can have an impact on your chances of success. So if an image shows you holding a drink, wearing a pink panther outfit at a Halloween party, it can count against you. 'In 2018, a majority of employers reported investigating social media sites to help them evaluate potential employees, and most of them eliminated candidates based on negative content,' said Michael Tews, associate professor of hospitality management, citing a recent report by CareerBuilder. 'It is important for job candidates to be aware of how they portray themselves in social media' [5].

Another recruiter confirms that the presence of social media is an important factor in hiring. 'It is the recruiting world we live in now,' says Matt Lanier, a corporate recruiter at Eliassen Group, 'If the candidates are willing to publicly post something on social media, a potential employer has every right to factor it in when considering you for a job' [6].

It is a great feeling to be 'liked' or to have lots of 'friends' online, but that is not the crucial point in hiring. Companies want to see how a person can build relationships and connect with influencers, industry leaders and organizations from their field. In a job, if a person knows how to use social media as a tool to interact, network and create an image of an intelligent responsible adult, it can even help them.

This places pressure on the jobseeker to create a positive image on social media. And if you are looking at other people's posts, those who are on a similar career path, it can be discouraging to see that they are more successful. So, to play it safe, you may choose to avoid sharing content on social media. But that might not work either. In fact, in a competitive job environment, you might not stand out to a potential recruiter. A person who shares their successes and connections may be favoured for the job.

This then raises the fact that people naturally differ in how much they share. Some are more outgoing and bold. They might enjoy being in the spotlight. However, others are more modest and reticent about sharing anything at all. They may put a higher premium on privacy and are not inclined to boast their successes or loudly announce their triumphs. They are equally talented and skilled, but their choices are different in how they project themselves to the world. We don't know who is telling the truth about themselves and who is not. And we end up competing with an unreal person.

Devidasani notes that we have a natural tendency to compare our lives with others. 'If someone is already dissatisfied with a specific aspect of their lives, they may be envious or jealous of others who seem to have it great. For instance, someone just quit their job because they were unhappy. If they see a post of their peer who got a job at a better company, they may have thoughts like "I am not competent enough to get a job at such a good company." Or "Should I have just stuck to my old job?" Insecurity, self-doubt and negative automatic thoughts start to creep in when we compare ourselves with someone who seemingly is at a better position.'

## BOUNDARIES IN COMMUNICATIONS

With the advent of easy access to the internet via mobile phone technology, we are engulfed by this new way of social media communication. One of the biggest changes in the way we interact, due to social media networks, is the sheer number of people we can interact with. Thousands of people all over the world are accessible in an instant. This kind of accessibility is the norm, the point is how much does it help or hamper the quality of life.

At the workplace, one would imagine that it is inappropriate to allow employees to check their social media feeds. It is important to recognize the value of social media as it has become a relevant aspect of our lives. Studies reveal that enabling access to social media at the workplace can be a morale booster. It can improve job performance and trust. It is great for improving communication across multiple offices and to keep in touch remotely. If a company encourages its employees to connect via social media, it will make it easier for them to get to know each other and build relationships in a supportive and positive way [7].

Companies are receptive to change and are aware that many small allowances can improve teamwork, employee engagement and make people a lot happier and loyal to the company. They feel as if they are part of a supportive community.

Social media gives employees much-needed breaks from intensive work. It offers a means for recognizing employee successes and allows people to connect professionally. It is a way to keep a good rapport between the management and employees. LinkedIn as a professionals' platform is where many people share articles to improve in various areas in the workplace. One can develop and understand from multiple perspectives.

Communication was the main purpose of the invention of social media. It is still very much a useful tool, but it has led to miscommunication in many ways.

Online communication tends to fall short when compared to face-to-face communication. An estimated 60–70 per cent of human communication takes place non-verbally. When the non-verbal side is missing, we experience awkward misunderstandings. This can be a problem not just for work but also for personal communications, as we increasingly rely on text and e-mail rather than phone or meeting in person.

Two Hong Kong-based students, Ivy and Angela, shared their experiences pertaining to the use of social media. They mention that when they are online, they are unable to benefit from certain body language expressions. They note that virtual communication is less clear

> like a blanket covering true emotions. In real life, we can tell if someone is faking a smile. Online, it takes just

two taps to send a smiley icon, and no one can tell if it is sincere. As a result, online relationships hold less truth, trust, commitment, and value. [8]

Dr Allen Dorcas is a Counselling Psychologist and Senior Teaching Fellow at the Hong Kong Polytechnic University. He explains that in social media sharing platforms, where there is no real face-to-face connection with others, sharing happens without various helpful cues that are available when the person is in front of us. This social interaction online is more robotic and can lead to people feeling that they are not truly seen or understood, leading to greater self-doubt and fear of not being accepted. Users commonly check on the number of 'likes' and 'shares' to validate their self-worth, and this is not a very sound way of building strong self-acceptance and self-esteem. Real connection and real sharing with empathy allow us to feel heard, understood and accepted, and this can help boost self-esteem [9].

Devidasani suggests that healthy limits are essential in online relationships. Sharing too much, too quickly about your personal life to strangers can blur personal boundaries, making them more porous. And porous boundaries make it easier for external influences—positive or negative—to creep in. For example, people take criticism too personally or are too easily swayed by intellectual opinions. All of these external factors cause us to see ourselves through the lens of others. Our self-worth weakens and becomes dependent on others.

## MINDFUL OF RELATIONSHIPS

Minal Mahtani is a Hong Kong-based counsellor and cognitive behaviour therapist. She says that self-esteem is often affected by family, social and cultural factors [10]. Traumatic incidents can also influence self-esteem. However, she affirms that social media also has an impact on the self-esteem of many adults and young people. 'They tend to base their worth on the number of "likes" that they receive and evaluate themselves in that light. This happens if people don't have a strong sense of self, or if they are struggling with self-esteem issues or identity issues.'

She adds that from another perspective, social media posts can be an outlet for them to express themselves and experience their sense of worth. However, it is important that they don't evaluate their posts on the basis of the reaction of others. Mahtani notes that healthy self-esteem needs to be cultivated by accepting one's strengths and acknowledging flaws. One should be able to accept others' talents without comparison to themselves.

On social media, people are habitually scrolling through selfies directly leading to comparisons or envy. People with low self-esteem also depend more on social media to feel temporarily better about themselves. The 'likes' and comments give them a sense of belonging and acceptance. They may use social media to prove to themselves that their self-image is not so negative in reality. This dependency is not a healthy way of coping because they fail to address their core beliefs.

Social media and technology have added a whole new dimension to dating and relationships. Devidasani says that the quality of a relationship is adversely affected. When a relationship is formed purely online, the essence of a true connection is lost.

> 'You're simply talking to a screen and not the person behind it. Technology is becoming a replacement for meeting people face-to-face, building real relationships and having a wholesome experience of being truly present with someone special in the moment. Emotions

are expressed through emojis and gifs. Besides, people are expected to be available online all the time. If a relationship is uncertain and insecure, it could lead to people requiring constant validation and reassurance from their partner. This can manifest into constant texting and calling throughout the day with no regard for one's personal space. This is not to say that this kind of dependence on a partner would not exist without technology, but increased access does make it harder to maintain healthy boundaries.'

Joanna experienced a different dynamic when she was looking to get into a relationship. Her friend suggested online dating. She swiped through hundreds of faces before agreeing to meet someone, essentially a stranger. After a few successful dates, she was 'ghosted'. The man disappeared suddenly. He didn't respond to Joanna's messages, and she ended up feeling horrible. In countless cases, online dating has left individuals in a heartbroken state.

It's been scientifically shown that online dating wrecks self-esteem.

Another self-esteem killer on the dating scene is 'breadcrumbing'. The *New York Times* describes it as follows: 'They communicate via sporadic noncommittal, but repeated messages—or breadcrumbs—that are just enough to keep you wondering but not enough to seal the deal. Breadcrumbers check inconsistently with a romantic prospect, but never set up a date' [11].

Feeling rejected is a common part of human experience, but that feeling ends up becoming even more intense and disturbing when it comes to digital dating. It can multiply the destruction that rejection has on our psyches, according to psychologist Guy Winch, PhD, who has given TED Talks on the subject. 'Our natural response to being dumped by a dating partner or getting picked last for a team is not just to lick our wounds, but to become intensely self-critical,' wrote Winch in a TED Talks article [12].

Despite the technological ease with which we can connect, many adults are lonely. Social media has emerged as a suspected cause of this phenomenon. If technology is making Millennials and Generation X the most connected generations, is it also making them the most lonely generations?

Devidasani suggests that social media is not a direct cause of self-isolation and loneliness. It could be that increased self-isolation tendencies cause more social media use or vice versa. A relationship formed purely online might not be as meaningful and profound as a relationship formed offline. Replacing meaningful offline relationships with relatively superficial online ones may lead to greater loneliness and lower well-being.

Two students of an international school in Hong Kong shared that the faceless majority on the internet lack identity. 'The presence of the Internet has made us more connected than ever before; however, the vast number of users has made us lonelier. As a result, our voice is less heard among the sea of similar voices.'

Genuinely connecting with people is becoming increasingly difficult. People differ in their thoughts, feelings, values and styles of communication. Misunderstood messages, whether offline or online, can prompt reactions that cause misunderstandings. Particularly in the case of electronic communication, what is unstated can be greater than what is directly expressed. How do you bond with a person online? And how much of what that individual share is true? We are driven instinctively to be cautious. After Joanna was traumatized from heartbreak for the first time, she found it hard to trust another date again.

Today, countless dating websites are available. Devidasani shared a view that people find it easier to end relationships because many more potential partners can be found online. This can lead to rebound relationships, which is another unhealthy way of coping with a failed relationship.

There are many individuals online who construct and share fake identities. When we begin to realize that we are being manipulated online and finally begin to see someone for who they are, we feel confused and angry. It is painful to learn the truth. We wonder why someone would behave in this way. We feel shame because we were conned, and we are wracked with the question 'Was it me that messed up?' This can lead to increased anxiety, and we end up overanalysing, misinterpreting or trying to fathom the reasons for someone to be so cruel.

Devidasani added that you may have a wonderful conversation online, but when you meet face-to-face, you may not have anything to talk about. So what one is getting to know is the constructed self that the other is trying to portray. This often leads to conflicts, emotional abuse, gas lighting, disappointments and ultimately failed relationships.

Pain and self-doubt can spill over into future interactions. On the next date, the person will constantly read between the lines of every post and comment. Being on the defensive side to protect our hearts can become an automatic habit. One will dwell on the incident and try to make sense of how this could have happened. However, it is not possible to understand the real reason for someone behaving in an untrustworthy way.

Dr Suzana Flores, a psychologist and author of *Facehooked*, shares,

> Interactions with emotionally manipulative personality types can seriously affect your emotional well-being. Through your interactions with them you may become fearful and depressed, but feel that you cannot let them

go. You may notice that you apologize a lot to them or that you've changed your own behaviour around them. You've probably also grown accustomed to making excuses for them or tried to help them because, on a certain level, they've convinced you that their behaviour is your fault. [13]

Social media creates global connectedness, greater sharing of life events and dating ease; but it can create lower self-esteem, social stalking and what Behavioural Scientist and Relationship Coach Clarissa Silva calls 'vanity validation'. She says that we have two selves, the real and the digital. The self that we share on social media seeks validation [14].

## SELF-EVALUATION AND COMPARISON

We all know that sense of disquiet that tends to bubble up inside of us when we scroll through hundreds of social media feeds of people more successful than us. It provokes us to think and wonder and to wish upon many improvements in our lives. There is envy or regret, there is a sense of bitterness too. A whole spectrum of emotions spreads through us. The one that sticks the most is 'Are we good enough compared to...?' we ask.

This tendency to compare ourselves to others is a habitual way of measuring our successes and failures. It is natural, and it is not easily switched off. We are often caught up in comparison that we fail to step back and realize just how unrealistic these comparisons are. To be sure, a comparison is a fundamental human tendency. But in the age of social media, comparison can quickly become unhealthy. Social media has become a tool for parading the best. This makes comparisons arbitrary and severe. Not all comparisons are necessarily problematic. Measuring ourselves against others can be informative and beneficial. Someone else's achievements can inspire and motivate us. But, on the whole, comparisons leave us feeling discouraged and inferior.

'Comparison is part innate, part learned,' says UK's first comparison coach, Lucy Sheridan, who is the author of *The Comparison Cure*. 'We rank children at school and praise individuals with gold stars, all of which makes us feel in competition with others rather than with ourselves at a very early age' [15].

Psychologist Leon Festinger proposed the theory of social comparison in 1954. According to social comparison theory, individuals determine their own social and personal worth on the basis of how they measure against others. Comparisons are made upwards and downwards. Upward social comparison with those who we perceive as better in some way makes us feel worse about ourselves. The downward social comparison makes us feel better. Social media magnifies the impact of social comparison on our wellness.

Besides that, researchers have found that people who spent significant time viewing photos of Facebook friends later reported reduced self-esteem. We are highly susceptible to reactions from our social connections; the more we are accepted and liked, the more we satisfy our need to be accepted in a group [16]. Allowing ourselves to be consumed by peoples' constructed lives is the result of this connected society that we have created for ourselves.

Social media itself isn't necessarily the problem; it is this obsession with our social media image that creates the problem. We end up upgrading our own choices against other people's decisions, often referred to as analysis paralysis, which means that when we have to make major life decisions, we tend to get stuck.

Devidasani states that no one posts fights, failures, sad moments or challenges. They post their exotic vacations, gifts received, the expensive car they just bought, airbrushed versions of themselves and romantic gestures, to name a few.

We are comparing our difficult reality with someone else's fake reality. This can hurt our self-esteem, making us feel inadequate and insecure about our lives.

We evaluate our work performance, relationship status, body size and even our athletic ability on the basis of standards set by others. Studies show that men who compare themselves to muscled male physiques evaluate their body negatively. Young women face the same pressure and stress when comparing themselves to fashion and media models. Teenagers tend to focus on qualities such as perceived attractiveness and popularity when they engage in social comparison. Furthermore, they may compare their abilities and skills, such as sports ability or artistic talent.

Dr Dorcas explains that the current generation uses more external referencing to identify themselves. With increased dependence on external technologies, people are less in touch with themselves and more addicted to being validated by external means. Self-esteem comes from feeling good about ourselves, and this develops with safe and trusting relationships that reflect us that we are loved and valued. With greater use of social media and technology, we feel more separated from others. Accordingly, there is less opportunity for validation and more room for self-doubt to creep in, leading to low self-esteem.

He adds that social media tends to focus on certain specific images that are acceptable and praiseworthy. 'If you possess this appearance, you will be loved by others…if you have this product, you will be cool, and people will envy you…if you don't, you will be lacking and be less attractive.' These are the underlying beliefs that are fostered by social media. This is particularly the case with advertisements that are promoted on social media platforms. So we are constantly comparing ourselves with the 'ideal' and often falling short.

Dr Dorcas says, 'I believe that kids rely heavily on their peers and friends to identify themselves and learn to feel good or bad about themselves. These days, with less chance for social contact, except for online platforms, there can be a greater sense of isolation, not belonging and self-doubt. We are no longer able to validate ourselves through social interaction as we once did, and this can lead to greater feelings of being left out or separated from others'.

Studies have linked the effect of 'likes' on your brain to that of taking drugs for recreational pleasure. When users receive 'likes', the reward system in the brain is activated and releases dopamine, causing people to associate 'likes' with the same pleasure one may feel from taking narcotics [17]. On the opposite end of the spectrum, studies show that a lack of 'likes' is also linked to depression in some who feel they go unnoticed, are not important, and are not well liked [18].

Dr Jennifer Lewallen explains that social comparison is not always a bad thing.

> ...social comparison can benefit people who have high self-esteem. They tend to experience feelings of motivation or hope when engaging in upward social comparison. For example, you might follow a popular social media account where the person recently completed a marathon and posted an impossibly perfect post-race photo. For users who have healthy self-esteem, this may serve as an inspiration to try and achieve a goal like this. [19]

Not everyone cares about the 'likes' they receive. A 25-year-old hospital nurse, Mary Cheung, posts updates to share about others, about people who have survived through challenging illnesses, rather than using 'likes' to boost her self-worth. Cheung says, 'It's more of a way to see if people see what I see or understand what I do. For me, it's to connect with like-minded people.'

Since the way we communicate online is so significant, we need to monitor not just our thoughts and well-being but also our clicks and posts. The impression we create may affect others. If I keep glorifying how much we have achieved, I need to reconsider how the post impacts others who may feel they have not achieved much.

Avinash Sujanani says that YouTube has been a great influence on him, but he makes sure to keep tabs on how he feels while on social media. 'If I have self-doubt, I try to remember my "why" and purpose. This helps to motivate me when I am faced with self-doubt. Additionally, I try to get a pep talk from my mum or positive friends.'

He adds that social media can be dangerous if the person has thin skin. 'You feel a lot more powerful online than in person when communicating and confronting someone. You don't have to face the other person's reaction. When I was 12 years old, I got into an online argument with someone from my school. I said some things that I wouldn't have the courage to say in real life. Once I said it, I knew I had to face the consequences when I showed up to school. As a result, the outcome was not good.'

'Research shows that Generation Z has a far healthier relationship with the media than us,' explains Bea Arthur. The 'us' refers to Gen X and the Millennials in her TEDx Talk 'The Culture of Comparison'. 'They understand how damaging it can be and have been able to put limits and boundaries in place at an age when they're vulnerable and impressionable. We weren't and we're feeling the effects.' She shares that as we continue to delve and compare our lives to others, our happiness becomes a moving target. What once made us feel content is now not enough, and we end up feeling not good enough [15].

## BOTTOM LINE

The new 'Digital 2022 April Global Statshot' report revealed that, more than 5 billion people around the world actively use the internet [20].

It is clear that social media is a part of our lifestyle. It influences us in many different ways. The main one is that it is addictive. We want to get online to connect with others because we want to have a sense of belonging in certain groups or online communities that share similar interests. At times, this urge is just a simple desire to check in with friends, and other times it becomes unhealthy scrolling through hundreds of updates. We don't realize how much our minds are immersed and lost inside this online world. Some updates are positive. They motivate us to learn and to transform ourselves. However, other newsfeeds affect our state of mind which can lead to depression.

Researcher Morten Tromholt of Denmark found that, after taking a one-week break from Facebook, people had a higher life satisfaction and positive emotions compared to people who stayed connected [21].

Just like we prepare ourselves before a meeting, we should mentally prepare ourselves before checking social media. We need to be aware of the thoughts that crop up with each newsfeed. We must check in with our feelings while on social media. This will help to understand what causes reactions and what kind of feelings linger after we shut down the page. Are we upset? Frustrated? Feel like a failure? Observe the thoughts and detach from them. They only hinder your progress. Frankly, if we are going to live with social media all our lives, why should we let it decide how we feel about ourselves? We need to be in control, not let it control us.

Ideally, one should schedule time to step away from social media. Unplug often and go out for a walk or a face-to-face coffee with a friend. Talk about your negative feelings and let them go.

Be mindful of the purpose of logging in. If you feel the urge to make comparisons, compare your present self with your past self. And with a little bit of reflection, you can use other people's posts as a way to learn and be inspired.

'I believe everyone is on a journey from self-doubt to self-acceptance. The more we grow in loving who we are, the greater our self-esteem is and the less this inner critic will be a source of self-judgment and doubt,' says Dr Dorcas.

## REFERENCES

1. Office of University Relations. Twenge discusses mental health, social culture and the 'IGen' generation; 2019. Available from: https://www.utm.edu/news/2019/09/04/twenge-discusses-mental-health-social-culture-and-the-igen-generation/

2. Devidasani S. E-mail interview. Mumbai; 2020.

3. Steinmetz K. Instagram's challenge. Time; 2019.

4. Sujanani A. Phone interview. Hong Kong; 2020.

5. IANS. Want a good job? Don't express strong views on Facebook. Outlook; 2020. Available from: https://www.outlookindia.com/newsscroll/want-a-good-job-dont-express-strong-views-on-facebook/1727637

6. Thottam I. These social media mistakes can actually disqualify you from a job. Monster Career Advice; 2019. Available from: https://www.monster.com/career-advice/article/these-social-media-mistakes-can-actually-disqualify-you-from-a-job

7. Hughes A. Should you allow social media in the workplace? 5 pros and 5 cons. Coburg Banks; 2016.

Available from: https://www.coburgbanks.co.uk/blog/staff-retention/social-media-in-the-workplace/

8. Schmidt M. Technology and youth disconnect: perspectives from international school students. Social Conscience and Inner Awakening; 2014. Available from: https://martinschmidtinasia.wordpress.com/2014/08/29/technology-and-youth-disconnect-perspectives-from-international-school-students/

9. Dorcas A. E-mail interview. Hong Kong; 2020.

10. Mahtani M. Phone chat interview. Hong Kong; 2020.

11. Bennett J. The agony of the digital tease. The New York Times; 2016. Available from: https://www.nytimes.com/2016/07/10/fashion/dating-text-messages-bread crumbing.html?_r=2

12. Winch G. Why rejection hurts so much—and what to do about it. Ideas.Ted.com; 2015. Available from: https://ideas.ted.com/why-rejection-hurts-so-much-and-what-to-do-about-it/

13. Flores S. Facebook emotional manipulators—the psychological effect; 2014. Available from: https://drsuzanaflores.com/facebook-emotional-manipulators-the-psychological-effect/

14. Silva C. Vanity validation; 2017. Available from: http://clarissasilva.com/tag/vanity-validation/#:~:text=Many%20are%20experiencing%20it%2C%20but

15. Walker A. Comparison culture: impact of Instagram on our self-esteem. Stylist; 2020. Available from: https://www.stylist.co.uk/life/comparing-ourselves-to-others-comparison-culture-research-self-esteem-instagram-social-media-success-careers-fitness-relationships/345725

16. Baumeister RF, Leary MR. The need to belong: desire for interpersonal attachments as a fundamental human

motivation. Psychol Bull 1995;117(3):497–529. Available from: https://doi.org/10.1037/0033-2909.117.3.497

17. Chan M. The psychology of social media. Medium; 2016. Available from: https://medium.com/@MarshaChan/the-psychology-of-social-media-712222f07d1d

18. Beres D. 10 hidden negative effects of social media on your brain. The Healthy; 2018. Available from: https://www.thehealthy.com/mental-health/negative-effects-of-social-media/

19. Finnerty-Myers K. A scholar breaks down the real reasons we compare on social media. Darling; 2018. Available from: https://darlingmagazine.org/scholar-breaks-real-reasons-compare-social-media/

20. https://datareportal.com/reports/digital-2022-april-global-statshot

21. Tromholt M. The Facebook experiment: quitting Facebook leads to higher levels of well-being. Cyberpsychology Behav Soc Netw 2016;19(11):661–666. Available from: https://doi.org/10.1089/cyber.2016.0259

Life is demanding. We may find that our efforts leave us feeling incomplete. We adapt, we change and yet we feel that something is missing. We hustle to keep up with everyone else. When we are forced to follow arbitrary standards, we find ourselves off-track. We are immersed in a sea of information that makes life more complex. How we interact with this form of input and how it affects our willpower and personality depends on us. That is exactly why we need to gather our strength to be who we truly want to be.

At any time, we may lose track of our original vision of life. We chase after goals and external validation. The joy of achieving milestones is short-lived, but we ride the goal-seeking roller coaster again and again, endlessly grasping at straws. We lose sight of our passion while we compete and compare ourselves with others. It is time to find what makes us distinctive, what sets us apart and to embrace our unique qualities as our guiding star. We need to marshal our courage to bring our authentic self out into the world. We confront a choice to be defeated or to rise and try again.

We have created barriers between ourselves and others. If we are not able to accept others as they are, it is much harder to accept ourselves. If we compete, compare and criticize, we may become as bitter as those who envy us. Conversely, with self-love, our hearts expand to be more accepting of others.

By taking a fresh perspective, we can advance greater human connectedness, both within our local sphere and ultimately beyond. Our unique strengths and vulnerabilities can be complementary assets. Being committed to self-acceptance and compassion can help us realize our full potential and set the stage for greater human unity. Let us revive our instinctive capacity for empathy, to look within for answers, and let us embrace opportunities to expand our hearts to include others.

# CHAPTER 7

# FEARS OF BEING UNIQUE
## SOCIETY AND CULTURE

*True belonging and self-worth are not goods;*
*we don't negotiate their value with the world.*
*The truth about who we are lives in our hearts.*
*Our call to courage is to protect our wild heart*
*against constant evaluation, especially our own.*

—Brené Brown, Braving the Wilderness

### THE CROW AND THE PEACOCK

This is one of my favourite stories of classical Greek origin, usually ascribed to Aesop. It has been written in many different ways by many different cultures.

Once upon a time, there was a crow whose feathers were as black as coal. The crow despised his appearance, hated that it was black and was miserable because it felt ugly compared to other birds. Feeling out of sorts, it decided to roam around the cities. One day it saw a beautiful white swan. The crow perched on a nearby tree, in awe of the swan's stunning white feathers which shimmered in the sunlight. It decided to share its feelings with the swan. 'You are so beautiful and graceful, dear swan. You must be so happy and content.'

The swan looked at the crow with a glum expression, 'You are mistaken, dear crow. I am not happy with being plain white. I saw a sunbird with such a beautiful red plumage. I wish I had some kind of colour. I would think that the sunbird is the most beautiful and must be the happiest.'

The crow felt slightly better that it was not the only one who was miserable. It flew in search of the sunbird. When it saw the little bird perched on a tree, it was amazed by its beauty. The stunning feathers glimmered among the green leaves. When the crow shared its admiration, the sunbird responded, 'No you are mistaken. I was very happy with my glorious red feathers until I saw the peacock. What an amazing array of colours! I am nothing compared to the peacock!' The sunbird flitted away.

The crow was surprised and curious. It flew far and wide in search of the peacock. It finally saw the bird in a park enclosure. Many people were looking at it. The crow hovered on the fence, watching the peacock dance elegantly, bowing and fanning its feathers while the people took photos. The crow felt that the peacock must be so proud and arrogant because of its beauty. It was indeed ravishing. The crow hesitated and called out, 'Beautiful peacock! I see you have many admirers. You are indeed the king of the birds. Your feathers are a delight, and your beauty is astounding. You must be the happiest bird in the world!' The crow went on to say in a glum voice, 'My feathers are as black as night, and no one wants to gaze and admire me. I am the ugliest bird. It is so depressing; no one likes me. Humans even call me a bad omen.'

The peacock looked at the crow, downcast, and said, 'You are right I am the most beautiful and fabulous bird, and my feathers are highly prized. It is a wonderful compliment to be recognized with such admiration. You would think that I would be so happy and elated, but alas such is not the case!' The peacock sighed, 'Because of my beauty, I cannot roam free. I am trapped within this boundary of a park.

You are free and able to fly around. I am very sad to be stuck here, dear crow. I think you must be the happiest bird to be able to go anywhere you wish and be free of these constraints.'

The moral of this story is clear. No one is satisfied with their lives. Comparisons make us desire more respect, a different face, body and bank balance because we choose not to accept what we possess. Others are probably looking at us with that same thought: 'He or she must be so happy. They have everything perfect...' And when you talk to those who seem to have it all, they are often dissatisfied with some aspect of their lives. 'If only I had this or that I would be happy.' Everyone is unique and yet everyone wishes they could walk in someone else's shoes.

The idea of making the world a smaller place also means accepting different cultures and people, just as we accept ourselves. With our current high ideals, we might expect everyone to embrace the idea of one human family. But divisions persist. Not everyone thinks the same way. It is no surprise that there is more dissonance than harmony in society. And not just in society, but within ourselves. We struggle as we find our beliefs in tension with our external life.

We are unique in terms of the way we view the world from our experiences and belief systems. That is why I keep referring to Leon Festinger's notion of cognitive dissonance. It describes the unease within us when our actions and thoughts are not in sync, that is, when our beliefs don't match our behaviour.

Why is it relevant? It's because when we engage in uncomfortable behaviour, we push ourselves to fit into a belief system or group that does not resonate with us. Examples are when you are not a drinker but have to drink to be part of a group. Or when you own a small car but feel the pressure to own a bigger one. If you submit to the pressure by having that extra glass of wine or working extra hard so you can buy a bigger car, the guilt lingers.

Cognitive dissonance is not necessarily bad. In some cases, it motivates one to change bad habits, for example, eating healthy or engaging in regular physical exercise. Therefore, whichever way you look at it, dissonance makes us consider new patterns of thinking to make certain choices without feeling guilt and pressure.

The point is that whatever you choose to do, do it for your own reasons, not to live up to someone else's ideals.

Our feelings are a result of our thoughts. Whenever we are in conflict with our 'shoulds', we suffer. We betray our gifts and inspiration by making someone else's choice ours. Many times, these kinds of thoughts relate to some unhealthy beliefs from childhood. Usually, it is a parent who makes the child feel that he or she is bad. Those feelings stay with us.

In the previous chapters, I talked about the many interlinked traits that affect our self-esteem. It has become even more essential to stay grounded, to be firm and to have a sense of worth. As adults, we need to figure out how to avoid getting our self-esteem gut-punched by external factors. If we pave the way for inner stability and awareness of our qualities, we will discover our true purpose.

To get there, let's first take a step back and understand self-esteem on a deeper level.

Steve Roberts is a psychology major from the University of Toronto. In response to a query about the meaning of self-esteem, he says that 'when we use made-up words, psychological terms to describe an extremely complex organism, one with mechanisms that are often invisible to us, as a result, a number of terms are imprecise.' It is complicated to describe a particular human behavioural trait accurately which over time is influenced and affected by many factors. To refer to the concept of self-esteem, he suggests that we must first understand that this word is a human-made construct.

It may not do justice to the concept of self-esteem in terms of human behaviour.

> Self-esteem is subjective, and it has been created to refer to the difference between one's *current* self-image and one's *ideal* self-image. 'Esteem' is related to 'estimation', so when we compare who we think we are or who we want to be, we are estimating the value of our current self. If the gap between current and ideal self is high, we have estimated our self to be low, so we have low self-esteem. If the gap is narrow, we have higher self-esteem. [1]

This becomes relevant because the levels of self-esteem fluctuate. When we push ourselves to fit into different situations that seem to be ideal due to external markers, we do not achieve our fullest potential. We try to fit in because we want to be accepted into a group or society. We do this because we feel that our unique personality will be ridiculed and we fear embarrassment or failure. We have feelings of inferiority.

Social media, imposter syndrome, high expectations, perfectionism, self-criticism and discrimination are just a few of the many ways in which self-esteem is dampened. Our thoughts and actions are constantly under scrutiny and analysis. If we are highly sensitive to external influences, and if we allow the influence to inhabit our inner world, then we put ourselves through daily torture and, worst of all, we lose our uniqueness. Feeling inferior every day is not a pleasant lifestyle for anyone.

James E. Maddux, PhD, psychologist and author of *Subjective Well-Being and Life Satisfaction* and co-author of *Psychopathology: Foundations for a Contemporary Understanding* explains that the inferiority complex is an old-fashioned term for what he instead calls chronic low self-esteem. 'You call yourself names, lament your shortcomings, and believe that your intense self-criticism is reasonable. Just when your self-esteem is most fragile, you attack it even further. This cycle is so deeply rooted that it consistently holds you back personally and professionally' [2].

## FEELINGS OF INFERIORITY

The commonly accepted definition of an inferiority complex is a feeling that one is in some way inferior to others. It is deeply instilled and often subconscious. At times, it is thought to drive afflicted individuals to overcompensate, resulting in spectacular achievement.

According to the American Psychological Association, Alfred Adler coined the terms 'inferiority complex' and 'superiority complex' to refer to an 'exaggerated opinion of one's abilities and accomplishments'.

Superiority complexes are usually formed in reaction to feelings of inferiority, where people who show symptoms of superiority complexes are usually doing so to overcompensate their deep feelings of inadequacy [3].

Do you still hear your father or mother's voice in your head telling you that you will not succeed in life if you don't study hard, or a teacher berating you, telling you if you don't get into a prestigious university, or if you don't get the appropriate degree, you will never get a job? Do you feel guilty or responsible when your lover breaks up with you? Do you feel crushed when your colleague gets a promotion and you don't? Do you feel like a failure when your boss praises someone else but not you?

So many of these factors play on the mind as an automatic response, and if they are deeply rooted, they add pressure on our self-esteem. Even if we succeed in all the ways that we are expected to, there may still be a sense of dissatisfaction and restlessness, a feeling of 'still not good enough' that steals joy from life.

Let's face it. Everyone is inferior to someone else in some way. It could be a skill, appearance, status, class or even education level. If we move the focus from the external to the internal, to our capacity, our potential, we realize that we have a lot to offer.

Our feelings of inferiority often arise from our interpretations of situations, not facts. An important point to realize is that everyone is unique in their way of thinking, perceiving and reacting to the world. If we are trying to fit into a mould or live up to arbitrary standards set by someone else, we are upsetting our inner balance.

When this happens to a population, we end up losing ourselves in the sea of negativity. We compare rather than inspire, criticize rather than support and judge rather than empathize. Different sectors of our society tend to communicate about whose face or status fits in where. We are subject to labels, and we aspire to be in tune with others. We tend to be either too hard or too soft on ourselves. In some ways, our modern, smaller world tends to accentuate our differences instead of our commonalities.

The main reason we behave this way is the fear of standing out and being different because we believe that the world is so unforgiving. We would rather crush our desires and uniqueness than bear the possibility of being ridiculed.

To some extent, we can change the status quo, but most of us are small cogs in big wheels and to add to the mix we have to deal with luck, genes, politics and economics. All of these factors play a part in how easy it is to succeed or fail in today's fast-moving world.

We know that by taking responsibility for our thoughts and reactions, we give ourselves the power to make a change. Blaming luck or genes for our failures is a defeatist attitude that doesn't help us. Rather than focusing on negatives and psychological baggage, we can focus on achievements and persist with courage and face the fear.

## DEEP-ROOTED COPING MECHANISMS

Sonia Samtani is the founder of the All About You Centre in Hong Kong, featuring therapy, transformational workshops and other methods to support those in need. She has been practising hypnotherapy, coaching and training for over a decade and has developed her own techniques and healing modalities. Her vision is to empower individuals with simple yet powerful tools to heal past issues while they face their current dilemmas.

Samtani explains that our self-esteem is directly related to our self-acceptance. If we feel accepted by others and accept the way we are, the by-product is *feeling good enough*. When we feel inadequate, we overcompensate and get into fight or flight coping mechanisms. Fight mechanisms include arrogance and wanting to prove that we are good. Flight mechanisms are withdrawing, pretending we don't care and being scared to stand out. These crisis coping mechanisms have an evolutionary origin. In primitive times, they protected us from immediate physical threats, such as being chased by an animal. Nowadays, similar responses arise when we feel rejected or feel like a failure. Again, our instincts put us into fight or flight mode [4].

In his book *The Science of Self Talk*, Ian Tuhovsky says that the way we think still relies '…on the Palaeolithic, hunter-gatherer cognitive toolkit for navigating life, a lifestyle that no longer resembles what it is today. The threats and stressors are numerous: losing a job, losing face, losing in relationships, losing to a competitor, losing in investments' [5].

This way of thinking is commonly referred to as the primate or lizard brain, which is focused on survival.

When you are facing a situation or experience that overwhelms you, it is the voice in your head that tells you to be careful, back off, run away from danger and play it safe. The safety factor prevents you from taking risks and accomplishing goals in life.

The good news is that there are ways to overcome the fear and survival instincts of the lizard brain. We can learn to adapt and discover new ways to tackle our self-doubt. Then we can accept that we are good enough. Self-acceptance does not mean being complacent. This feeling that we are good enough comes from feeling worthy. It is not a crime to feel okay with oneself.

Samtani conveys that 'some people go as far as to think that if you say you are good enough, it means you are "big-headed" and they deny themselves the opportunity of feeling good. Others think they need to show that they are better than others in order to be "good enough" and validated. One of these options puts down the self in relation to others, while the other puts down others in relation to the self. In order to maintain high self-esteem in a healthy environment, we need to be in a space where we acknowledge both ourselves and others with equal respect.'

Samtani points out that while self-esteem is truly believing that you are enough the way you are, arrogance is trying to convince others that you are better than them.

At times, because of a fragile self-esteem, we take credit for an achievement but blame bad results on someone else. This comes from the fear of inadequacy. Certain individuals, when praised, will say, 'I planned ahead, I worked all through the night', or 'I was excited about the project'. However, when a negative evaluation is made, the individual may respond defensively, 'I had limited time.'

Another way to bypass responsibility is blaming someone else for your lack of self-esteem. Some psychological approaches encourage us to blame our mothers for all our flaws. But it is an easy way out. At the end of the day, we are responsible for our thoughts and feelings. If you talk about blaming your mother, you should consider that her environment, her family and her siblings, even the society, too, were responsible for her personality. As much as we may want to blame our parents or society for their low self-esteem, at some point we do need to take responsibility to change.

Jonathan was nervous before going for his job interview. He shared his experience with his roommate. The way he rationalizes is to say that the 3-person interview panel was stern, and one of the men kept looking at his watch, ignoring his words, making him nervous. Jonathan blamed them for his anxiety during the interview and implied that for things to improve in his life, other people have to change.

But if Jonathan took some time to reflect on the situation, he may realize that taking responsibility to hone his skills would be a better way of dealing with the situation. He could learn from his mistakes. He might even be able to make the interviewers sit up and show more interest in him. The point is that at times we need to do the best we can, and then say okay, it was not meant to be.

Reflecting honestly on our flaws is difficult. We are often defensive or afraid to admit that we can make mistakes. Our upbringing almost always makes us ashamed of our weaknesses. But only through these failed attempts can we learn. And, in a way, it is a test of our inner strength to persist through each obstacle in life.

Another way we undermine our potential is through perfectionism, putting up a front and hiding our vulnerabilities. When being perfect is the top priority, there is often an inclination called self-handicapping, where a perfectionist may withdraw efforts needed for a goal. The idea is that the person may feel that there is a greater threat to self-esteem if one tries and fails than if one does not try.

## INDIVIDUALISTIC AND COLLECTIVISTIC

Marc Reklau, author of *Love Yourself First! Boost Your Self-esteem in 30 Days*, says, 'Over the years I have seen people making quantum leaps and reaching their greatest goals by just making one single adjustment: raising their self-esteem.' He adds, 'As individuals and members of a specific culture, we are continually selecting and editing experience, creating an ego-based ideal of self and world' [6, 7].

Most research and theory on self-concept and self-esteem are based on Western cultures and populations; however, more attention is being paid to cross-cultural differences. For example, in collectivist cultures, such as those of Japan or China, the values and impressions of one's family, work group or peer group are the primary sources of self-esteem. By contrast, in more individualistic Western cultures, personal attributes and independence based on individual achievement may be more important for self-esteem.

In terms of self, there is considerable variation *within* each culture too. For example, within the USA and other Western countries, women are more likely to have an interdependent self-concept and men are more likely to emphasize an independent self-concept [8].

As the world populations interact and communicate with each other, cross-cultural psychology has become a relevant branch of psychology that looks at cultural factors that influence human behaviour. Our work culture is diverse with people from different parts of the world working within a shared environment. While many aspects of human thought and behaviour are universal, cultural variation can lead to many surprising differences in how people think, feel and act.

Social behaviour tends to be determined by the attitudes and preferences of individuals. Cultures in North America and Western Europe tend to be individualistic and, therefore, when Asians are working in such cultures, they have to adapt. Other cultures, however, place a higher value on cooperation among members of the group, which then can be a challenge for people who have a more individualistic nature. In such cultures, relationships with other group members and interconnectedness between people play a central role in each person's identity [9].

People from individualistic nations typically score higher on measures of self-esteem than people from collectivistic nations. They are also more likely to boast about their achievements when given the opportunity. People from collectivistic nations place a high value on self-criticism and self-improvement rather than self-esteem [10].

Hofstede Insights is a research group that provides information on organizational culture, intercultural management and consumer trends. The results from their cultural survey of India are surprising. One might imagine that India would score very high as a collectivistic culture [11].

However, their data show that:

> India is a society with both collectivistic and individualist traits. The collectivist side means that there is a high preference for belonging to a larger social framework in which individuals are expected to act in accordance to the greater good of one's defined in-group(s). In such situations, the actions of the individual are influenced by various concepts, such as the opinion of one's family, extended family, neighbours, work group and other such wider social networks that one has some affiliation to. For a collectivist, to be rejected by one's peers, or to be thought lowly of by one's extended and immediate in-groups, leaves him or her rudderless and with a sense of intense emptiness. Employer/employee relationship

is one based on expectations: loyalty by the employee and almost familial protection by the employer. Hiring and promotion decisions are often made on the basis of relationships that are key to everything in a collectivist society.

This kind of conditioning is a normal part of daily life in India but, in addition to this, there is an individualistic aspect to human culture which is also interesting.

> The Individualist aspect of Indian society is seen as a result of its dominant religion/philosophy—Hinduism. The Hindus believe in a cycle of death and rebirth, with the manner of each rebirth being dependent upon how the individual lived the preceding life. People are, therefore, individually responsible for the way they lead their lives and the impact it will have upon their rebirth. This focus on individualism interacts with the otherwise collectivist tendencies of the Indian society....

Communal religious philosophy is founded on the acceptance of one's fate, and yet the ability to stay grounded is an individualistic thought process. This indicates that no matter how much you are influenced by external factors, ultimately you have to learn to live within yourself. Your thoughts and choices are under your control. Over time, we can learn to manage our reactions.

Whatever our world or culture, everyone at some point in time, even the most famous individuals, has struggled with self-doubt and self-esteem. Yet their inner GPS has guided them to go forward, challenge their fears and push forward. We all have that in us. We just need to get through the layers of fear and distrust to find that faith within.

Researchers have indicated that when we are ignored by those whose attention we value, the physiological response in the brain is similar to physical pain. While this may be true in some cases, the fact is that there are different types of personality and each one responds differently. For example, if a boss speaks to an employee, some may appreciate it, and others may find it tiresome and interfering. Then some respond well to constructive criticism, and others lose their morale and fall apart. No single approach is right or wrong. This just goes to show that ultimately we are responsible for maintaining our inner strength.

## MAPPED IN CHILDHOOD

Children are vulnerable to the behaviours of the adults around them. And the messages children hear become internalized in their inner conversation. As a result, self-esteem issues start from a very young age.

Early child–parent interactions affect a person's representations of who they are, their self-worth and self-concept [12].

As parents, we feel that praising a child will make him or her happy and contribute to his or her future wellness. But heaping praise doesn't always help and might harm, according to Jim Taylor, author of *Your Children Are Listening: Nine Messages They Could Hear from You.* Self-esteem also comes from developing competence which, Taylor says, takes time and effort. Confidence comes from trying and failing, which helps the child to understand his or her strengths and weaknesses. Telling your child that he or she is the best and the smartest does not prepare him or her for the hard knocks of life [13].

Learning to make choices, such as taking responsibility to help around the house or running errands, increases their sense of value. Another way is to help the child follow his or her interest. For example, 10-year-old Anna developed an interest in origami, the Japanese art of paper-folding. She found it difficult at times and was ready to quit. However, gentle encouragement to keep trying even after she struggled enabled her to feel the satisfaction of accomplishing her goal of creating a paper crane.

Many parents feel that when children struggle with social rejection or failure in sports or academics, they should offer blanket praise to help them feel better. In actuality, this is a critical opportunity to teach them that it's okay to fail, struggle and grow. Learning from mistakes is the norm but being perfect is not. Parents should show unconditional love, not the love based on a report card or athletic performance. Teaching them to set goals and to try again, even if they fail, is a great way to help them face challenges. Learning to forge ahead with a resolute and balanced mind is the key to facing adulthood courageously.

Adolescence is a difficult time for everyone. Physical and hormonal changes can be very challenging. At that age, teenagers become fixated on a physical attribute and make comparisons with unrealistic standards. They are generally quite sensitive to comments about their looks and overall image. Parents need to tread carefully, especially since anything that is said could be taken to heart.

In 2016, *Collins Dictionary* included 'snowflake' among its list of 'Words of the Year', defining young adults of the 2010s as a group 'less resilient and more prone to taking offence than previous generations', implying that they are too sensitive. This characterization has also been used for the Millennials, those born between the 1980s and the early 2000s, and for the more recent generation, Generation Z, who are currently in their late teens and early 20s.

Dr Sharyn Graham Davies is an associate professor of social sciences and public policy at Auckland University of Technology. She says that there are two ways to look at the 'snowflake' generation [14].

One meaning implies a confident or unique individual who can go and do anything they aspire to, and the other is they lose heart at the smallest problem.

'One of the ways is the idea that parents are so invested in their children that they raise them with such self-confidence and the notion that they are unique individuals and they can go and do anything they want,' she explained. 'So just like a snowflake, they have their own individuality that no one can compete with them because they are quite singular and unique.'

Interestingly, in common parlance in the USA, 'snowflake' does not have a positive meaning, it is the 'idea of a snowflake falling down and it quickly evaporates and melts, and so the meaning, in that interpretation of snowflake, is that Millennials now don't have any grit, or guts, or courage.'

Although different cultures may have varying views, Davies disagrees that the Millennials have an inflated view of themselves. 'For the vast majority of Millennials, they have a great amount of courage and a great amount of compassion and passion, and we see that across the globe,' she said.

Millennials, in fact, are considered to be the overachieving generation.

A new study by British researchers at the University of Bath published in *Psychological Bulletin* rejects the idea that Millennials are just a bunch of spoiled 30-somethings who procrastinate through life by doing the bare minimum. They are highly stressed because they work so hard.

Increased usage of social media, more rigorous academics and college admissions, as well as increased competition in the job market, are all factors causing young Millennials to put higher expectations on themselves and to feel the pressure from others. 'Although perfectionists have an excessive need for others' approval, they feel socially disconnected and such alienation renders them susceptible to profound psychological turmoil,' says the study [15].

Often, parents tell young adults that they can achieve anything they want if they are willing to work for it. Psychologists have suggested that some forms of 'anything is possible' advice have emerged from a misapplication of mindset research, which was developed by Stanford Psychologist Carol Dweck, and that mindset education has spread to classrooms around the world. This research proposes that praising children for effort, rather than performance, will increase academic performance. But a 2018 analysis found that while praising effort over ability may benefit high-risk or economically disadvantaged students, it does not necessarily help everyone. It is important that perfectionism not be emphasized.

'The problem lies in how these ideas are applied. While the trait of persistence can be incredibly powerful, advice should not be so romanticized that it leads to perfectionism. Instead, failures can be part of the growth process.' Suniya Luthar and Nina Kumar suggest in a research paper that for teens in wealthy pressure cooker communities, 'it is not the lack of motivation and perseverance that is the big problem. Instead, it is unhealthy perfectionism, and difficulty with backing off when they should, when the high-octane drive for achievements is over the top' [16].

Rachel Simmons, teacher and author of *Enough As She Is: How to Help Girls Move Beyond Impossible Standards of Success to Live Healthy, Happy, and Fulfilling Lives*, has observed a troubling spike in students who feel that they should be able to control the outcomes of their lives by hard work alone. When they succeed, they feel powerful and smart. But when they fall short of what they imagine they should accomplish, they are crushed by self-blame. The brutal, messy reality is that you can do everything in your power and still fail. And the conditioned belief that success is always within one's grasp is an unfair expectation. This is also experienced by minorities whose experience of discrimination and inequality teaches them that hard work doesn't always pay off. University of Chicago Professor Lauren Berlant calls this 'cruel optimism.' The college admission game promises meritocracy that rewards hard work with entrance to college or university, but admission scandals and low acceptance rates make it impossible. 'The culture has taught them that feeling less than overwhelmed means they're lazy, that how they perform for others is more important than what actually inspires them, and that where they go to college matters more than the kind of person they are' [16].

In recent years, Ivy League colleges have enrolled more students from wealthy families. They are predominantly educating these already privileged students. These elite graduates then dominate the highest paying jobs in the economy. A *Wall Street* ethnography observes that top bankers are recruited only from the Ivy League and other comparable elite schools such as MIT and Stanford [17].

Every aspect of unfairness in the world points to the fact that being mentally strong is the key to keeping your chin up and forging ahead. Such persistence not only enables us to adapt but also enables us to develop the skills needed to keep our self-esteem intact. We, most of all, need to be less of an enemy and more of a friend to ourselves.

## THE STURDY Gen Zs (BORN BETWEEN 1997 AND 2012)

Generation Z seems to be better adjusted than the Millennials. Gen Zs are also called digital natives because they grew up shaped by technology, and the internet is an integral part of their daily lives. Social media for Gen Z is not merely a space for passive consumption or connectivity. Online platforms have become a space for them to speak their minds and protest against injustice.

They keep abreast of global issues, and they are more open to diversity. Social media platforms provide Gen Zs with extensive opportunities to learn about global cultures. This, in turn, is attractive to organizations that seek to make a difference in the world. Gen Z youngsters are open-minded and have fewer issues with gender identities and are vocal about fighting gender discrimination. They tend to challenge the male stereotype of not expressing emotions and always projecting strength.

In fact, in almost every sphere of life, Gen Zs are increasingly visible agents of change who are comfortable in their own skin and often fiercely independent. They are breaking down stereotypes by proudly wearing, doing and being whatever makes them feel good [18].

In India, the traditional norm in life was to live with parents and then with a spouse or in-laws. This was considered the established path for many generations of Indians. However, Gen Z has been challenging the conventional route. As opportunities for Gen Z grow, they want freedom to explore different career paths, relationships and ways of self-expression. They are not afraid to experience the unknown. Life is an adventure, and they want to test the waters.

Tinder has conducted a study on young Indians between the ages of 18 and 25. It turns out that 'being myself' has been the highest value for several years. Other priorities, in order of importance, were making parents proud, building strong friendships, completing education, exploring the world and meeting new people. They would much rather accumulate experiences than collect assets. Gen Z Indians put great value on pursuing a career in a field that they are passionate about. And as far as relationships are concerned, they don't wish to commit long-term but prefer to date to understand themselves better. The highest priorities are to explore who they are and assert their independence. This is a heartening sign of a generation that has a sturdy self-esteem. They are courageous to follow their own beliefs [19].

## BOTTOM LINE

When you travel the path of constantly moulding yourself to fit in, you may end up feeling that you are still dissatisfied. All the striving, just so that you can conform, only adds a strain to the existing hustle and bustle lifestyle. There is both pressure and dissonance. Our inner world is at times chaotic because our outer world demands so much of us. When we trust our inner needs, we will find our life and work imbued with a natural unbounded flow that dissipates fear and pressure.

Self-discovery is a way to understand your talents and skills to help you stand out. Being true to yourself means choosing what resonates within you. You don't have to follow the herd.

Being unique means liking who you are, the way you are and then living through that feeling. We begin to see that comparisons and competition are the phantoms that we create in our minds.

Take hope from the innate strength of human nature. We all have scars and baggage from the past, but growth is in our DNA. When we achieve breakthroughs in growth, we may find that we feel more whole and less self-critical. Looking ahead is the way forward. The challenge is to learn from the mistakes and not to let them shame or embarrass us. We are not perfect beings but simple beings learning from life. We must trust our inner voice.

We can look within and reflect on who we want to become. But when we do that, we accept ourselves, our mistakes and everything. Facing our flaws is hard, but we are pursuing our dream. The task is to discover our deepest passions and have the courage to fulfil them.

Our inner compass will tell us when we are off-track when we are forcing ourselves to be something other than what we truly are. Let's not forget that our own deepest intuition is a tremendous asset. It invites all of us to let go of artificial self-conscious efforts.

It invites us to take responsibility for our growth.

With increasing courage, we can move forward to be who we truly want to be.

Steven Pressfield, author of *The War of Art: Winning the Inner Creative Battle*, says:

> We fear discovering that we are more than we think we are. More than our parents, our children, our teachers think we are. We fear that we actually possess the talent that our still, small voice tells us. That we actually have the guts, the perseverance, the capacity.

## REFERENCES

1. Quora. What is the difference between low self-esteem and inferiority complex?; 2017. Available from: https://www.quora.com/What-is-the-difference-between-low-self-esteem-and-inferiority-complex

2. Alberts N. Understanding the inferiority complex. Everyday Health; 2017. Available from: https://www.everydayhealth.com/emotional-health/understanding-inferiority-complex/

3. Wisner W. What is an inferiority complex? Talkspace; 2019. Available from: https://www.talkspace.com/blog/inferiority-complex-what-is/

4. Sonia Samtani. Interview. Hong Kong; 2020.

5. Tuhovsky I. The science of self talk. Columbia, SC: Createspace; 2017.
6. Reklau M. Love yourself first! Boost your self-esteem in 30 days; Malta: The Author; 2018.
7. Reklau M. Boost your self-esteem in 30 days: how to overcome low self-esteem, anxiety, stress, insecurity, and self-doubt. Malta: The Author; 2020.
8. Marriage and Family Encyclopedia. Self-esteem: culture: Ethnicity and self-esteem; n.d. Available from: https://family.jrank.org/pages/1477/Self-Esteem-Culture-Ethnicity-Self-Esteem.html#ixzz6ZDYC1nck
9. Kendra C. How different branches of psychology study the brain and behavior. Verywellmind; 2019. Available from: https://www.verywellmind.com/major-branches-of-psychology–4139786
10. Konrath S. Self-esteem, culturally defined. In: Cultural sociology of mental illness: an a-to-z guide. Thousand Oaks, CA: SAGE Publications; 2012.
11. Hofstede Insights. Country comparison; n.d. Available from: https://www.hofstede-insights.com/country-comparison/india/#:~:text=In%20Individualist%20societies%20people%20are
12. Orth U. The family environment in early childhood has a long-term effect on self-esteem: a longitudinal study from birth to age 27 years. J Personality Soc Psychol 2018;114(4):637–655. Available from: https://doi.org/10.1037/pspp0000143
13. Taylor J. Your children are listening: nine messages they need to hear from you. New York, NY: Experiment; 2011.
14. Small Z. Age of outrage: how the term 'snowflake' came to define a generation. Newshub; 2019. Available from:

https://www.newshub.co.nz/home/ageofoutrage/2019/03/age-of-outrage-how-the-term-snowflake-came-to-define-a-generation.html

15. Friday F. Millennials strive for perfection more than any generation—at a cost. Observer; 2018. Available from: https://observer.com/2018/01/millennials-strive-for-perfection-more-than-any-other-generation/

16. Simmons R. Tell kids the truth: hard work doesn't always pay off. Time; 2019. p. 20.

17. Markovits D. Less elite more equal. Time; 2019. p. 19.

18. The ASEAN Post. The new generation of social media; 2020. Available from: https://theaseanpost.com/article/new-generation-social-media

19. ET BrandEquity. Tinder study reveals Gen Z is driven by self-discovery; 2019. Available from: https://brandequity.economictimes.indiatimes.com/news/digital/tinder-study-reveals-gen-z-is-driven-by-self-discovery/67450944

## CHAPTER 8

# KNOW THYSELF
## HANDLING IDENTITY CRISIS

*The mind is a tool. The question is, do you use the tool or does the tool use you.*

—Zen Proverb

### A RING'S TRUE WORTH

Long, long ago, in a land of kings and queens, a young man, who was full of self-doubt, went to see a wise man and spoke of his distress. 'O great and wise soul, I have asked many for advice, but I still feel worthless and find that I have no good qualities. All my friends are making money, while I wonder what to do with my life. Everyone calls me a failure and a fool. Please guide me.'

The wise man paused, glanced at the youth and then said that he had an urgent task to deal with first. The wise man said, 'I will help you, but first, I need someone to run an errand for me. Will you do it?'

Feeling dejected that the wise man didn't help immediately, the youth murmured that he would agree to run the errand. The wise man gave him a ring with a sparkling gemstone. 'Go to the market and sell this ring. I have to pay off a debt. You must get as much as possible for it. Nothing less than a gold coin!'

The youth reluctantly agreed to do the task. He headed to the marketplace and went from vendor to vendor offering the ring. He spoke to many people. Many showed an interest, but when the youth said that he wanted at least a gold coin, they turned away. Some even laughed at him.

The youth felt like a failure and realized that he was a useless fellow after all. A kind elderly man explained to the youth that the ring wasn't worth that much, and the most he could offer was a silver coin or some bronze. The young man was tempted, but he recalled the wise man's instructions to not sell the ring for less than a gold coin. The youth sadly returned to the wise man and told him that the ring wasn't worth that much, just a silver coin.

'My son,' the wise man suddenly said, 'this is a very important point. Before trying to sell a precious ring, one should get it appraised. We should find out it's worth from an expert. Who better than a jeweller would know the ring's true value?'

The young man agreed to go. The wise man warned, 'Don't sell the ring, just get it appraised and come right back.'

The young man hurried to the jeweller. After careful examination, the jeweller weighed the ring on a scale. He turned to the youth excitedly and said, 'This is a rare piece. I can give you 50 gold coins now, but if you give me more time, I can take it for 66 gold coins.'

The young man was shocked. So many gold coins! He was thrilled. He thanked the jeweller and hurried back. The wise man listened to the young man's excitement.

Then the wise man patted his shoulder, 'Learn from this experience young man! You are like this precious ring—unique and valuable. Only an expert can appreciate your true worth. So why are you going to random people to find out what is your worth?' [1]

## KNOW YOUR PERSONALITY TYPE

We often let others decide our value. People are generally ignorant of our talents and skills, and attribute too little value to them. Relying on someone else's standard does not give us a true picture of our worth. We need to first esteem who we are and, to do that, we need to get to know ourselves. What are our characteristics? Are we introverted or extroverted? Athletic? Intellectual? Our traits help us to understand which direction to take in life.

Carl Jung proposed that there are four psychological types: sensing, intuition, thinking and feeling, and that these influence our personality [2]. Over time, assessments and typologies of personality traits have proliferated in varied forms. These are widely used to enhance self-knowledge and improve relationships and work performance. Many online personality tests can teach us to understand our strengths, weaknesses, emotional profile and even our general intelligence. Other tests help to identify our skills and suggest suitable careers. These help us to determine the best ways to be of service to others. Personality quizzes such as Myers-Briggs, Sixteen Personality Factors, Big Five and various IQ tests are among the most familiar ones.

Marty Schmidt has taught in the Humanities Department at the Hong Kong International School since 1990, developing innovative courses on humanities that involve community service. He says that there is an important link between identity and job satisfaction. 'If you are in a job that does not support or develop your true self, it is difficult to feel fulfilled.' He believes that the enneagram is a great personality typing tool for understanding how unique we are. It offers us the opportunity to explore whether our current job is a good fit. 'Intriguingly, the enneagram is not only a psychological tool that will help you find yourself but also a spiritual tool that will assist you in learning how to also let go of yourself, which all the spiritual traditions say is vital for becoming who you are meant to be.'

As Schmidt explains, the enneagram suggests nine types or styles of personality, each indicating a worldview or a way of acting. 'While all of us have all nine types within ourselves, each of us also has our particular approach to the world that is seen predominantly through one of these types. The premise is that we all grow up with a body–mind–heart imbalance based on our particular type of enneagram, and that this imbalance becomes the chief feature of our horizontal, ego-based life. The solution for each of the nine types is to recognize and let go of this strength/limitation and to open up to the vertical world of presence.'

While the enneagram is often associated with personal self-knowledge, it also offers real practical benefit for navigating challenges in the workplace and life in general [3].

We have heard and read about people who elected to follow a certain career path but then switched to another, realizing their initial goals were not ultimately what they wanted. Often, we follow what those around us suggest, without actually understanding whether it suits us. For some, career changes are radical.

David Brooks is a political and cultural commentator for the *New York Times*. In his 2015 'Opinion' column of 'The Moral Bucket List', he brings to light the unique perspective of how mankind's relationship with self-esteem is evolving.

He calls it the 'humility shift' whereby moral and spiritual accomplishments result in a richer inner life. He explains that a couple of decades ago, parents and teachers were constantly praising children. These youngsters have grown up in a culture that rewards those who boast about themselves, those who know how to market themselves, those who show strength and hard-heartedness. We are expected to broadcast our talents, awards and skills, and show how perfect we are. But, Brooks says, the people he ever admired were those who were honest about their vulnerabilities. They are able to face their imperfections, such as selfishness, cowardice or a hunger for approval. These wonderful people are able to realize this and feel shame, which leads to humility, which has been best defined as 'an intense self-awareness from a position of other-centeredness' [4].

Interestingly, there is a story of Dalai Lama shared multiple times. He was once asked about self-hatred. His response was that he was confounded by the concept. He couldn't fathom the possibility that one could loathe oneself. It simply did not make sense to him.

Paul Fulton is a clinical psychologist and co-editor of *Mindfulness and Psychotherapy*. He shares that the Tibetans apparently have no experience of self-criticism or low self-esteem. He questions whether it is experienced, but expressed differently in different cultures.

He points out that when we suffer from insecurity, and despite our accomplishments, we still feel that we are not good enough, this indicates that we are constantly living with an attitude that something is wrong with the 'self'. A highly accomplished person, despite receiving validation, will never be able to achieve a positive sense of self in this circle of insecurity. It is not a shameful failure to feel insecure or harbour self-doubt. It is part of human experience. We learn to let go of the unrealistic expectations and to be okay with the reality of ourselves and our shortcomings.

To understand further, we know that self-esteem is important because it heavily influences our choices and decisions. In other words, self-esteem motivates us to explore our full potential. Persons with higher self-esteem tend to be persistent in pursuing their personal goals and aspirations.

People with lower self-esteem are less likely to regard themselves as worthy of successful outcomes. They also tend to give up too easily and are considered to be less resilient in overcoming obstacles. People with low self-esteem may have the same kind of goals as people with higher self-esteem, but they are generally less motivated to pursue them.

The fact is that it is up to us to actively develop self-esteem if it is low, and to rein in self-esteem if it is too high. The reason for not having a very high self-esteem is that it can turn into a form of narcissism, and therefore a superiority complex. The way to stay balanced is to first admit the truth about ourselves and to identify our weaknesses and strengths. Introspection and self-awareness are critical.

If we constantly berate ourselves, linger in self-pity, we become obsessed with our fix-it process as if we are broken individuals. We also tend to think that people are focused on our failures and weaknesses, and that we are embarrassed and ashamed because we imagine that they secretly despise us. When this happens, it is harder to accept our positive qualities and we end up feeling like frauds.

Often, we follow the goals that other people have defined for us. We presume they are right, and their idea will work for us. Yet when we pursue these arbitrary goals, we may not feel the expected sense of satisfaction. Instead, we want to give up. There is a sense of restlessness and disorder. And we end up with feelings of guilt or failure. We become unsure of what we want. And we cast about exploring different activities to figure out what will bring a sense of purpose into our lives.

## IDENTITY CRISIS

We suffer from an identity crisis when we are unsure of who we are or our role in life, or when we feel that we don't know the 'real me'. This concept of identity crisis originated from developmental psychologist Erik Erikson, who proposed that the formation and growth of one's identity are not confined to teenage years but also unfold throughout adult life. At any age, our experiences and challenges can affect our identity [5].

At age 29, Leena's dream was to work in an organization that raises awareness of climate change. An opportunity came up with an NGO in South America. It was a real risk to leave her family and her country behind. She would also have to leave the security of her then high-paying job. Yet she took this opportunity in a faraway land, feeling instinctively that it was her path. Leena adjusted quickly to her new role in a group making a massive difference in addressing climate change. She was invigorated in her new environment and felt a renewed sense of purpose. She was contributing meaningfully, and this had a great impact on her esteem towards others and herself. While Leena was living and working there, she fell in love with a man who was in the recycling business. After a few months, he proposed to her and she accepted. Leena didn't realize how fast her life was changing. She was extremely happy with her married life. She continued working at the NGO while also attending to her new home with her husband. But her family back home wasn't exactly thrilled by her decision. They had expected her to return and marry someone within their community. However, Leena had no intention of going home. She felt settled and loved her new life.

Leena soon realized that relationships are about compromise and, despite some hiccups, she was gradually adjusting to her new normal. Soon she was pregnant. It was a huge change for her, and she missed her family back home. She became overwhelmed with the thought of being a mother. While she was going through her inner turmoil, her husband's business was facing trouble. Leena was not sure what to do and how she could help him. Her job at the NGO wasn't paying enough, and soon she had to stop working. Leena suddenly felt that maybe she had been rash in her decisions and had made some choices without thinking about long-term consequences. She missed her job and at times felt frustrated that she was no longer in control of her destiny. She could no longer make decisions spontaneously. Now facing the huge responsibility of motherhood, she felt the pressure of not being able to handle it.

Wracked with self-doubt, Leena analysed and criticized every past decision. This process played havoc on her self-esteem. She loved her husband and wanted everything to be perfect and yet she felt she had failed in her life. Her own family was disappointed in her. After her baby was born, her husband was extremely supportive and helped Leena to adjust. He helped her realize that she was capable and that he was there by her side. His family was genuinely kind and made her feel comfortable. Leena soon regained her self-esteem and focused on the joys of motherhood. She took this time as an opportunity to take up an online course to learn more about climate change and sustainability. Eventually, she would follow her career aspirations part-time and later partner with her husband in his business. For now, she was happy and motivated. She felt her current phase, in a way, enriched her life experiences [6].

Life requires compromises so that we can feel gratitude for the lessons of life. But when we are off course for a long time, a niggling part of us lets us know. We may feel a heavy weight of doubt and suspicion that another path could have given us greater fulfilment.

What does it feel like to experience an identity crisis?

You feel like a different person almost every day. Some people say that when they look in the mirror, they feel like they are looking at a stranger. Psychologists connect doubts about identity to childhoods. If we don't hit the right markers of psychological and emotional growth, we can become an adult who lacks a holistic idea of who they are [7].

All individuals have two types of identity: the social and the personal. Social identity relates to the roles that we have in our lives or the cultural groups that we belong to. Examples include engineer, professor, singer, Hindu and American. Personal identity relates to individual markers such as our likes and dislikes, goals, achievements, emotions, body image and behaviours. Self-esteem comes from your self-evaluation on the basis of your identity and self-image, influencing how you feel about yourself. If identity is repressed, this can directly affect self-image and lower self-esteem [8].

We have to figure out what makes us feel complete as a person. When we constantly see ourselves in a diminished light and presume that another person's path is also our path, we lose our unique spark. We continue to push ourselves towards a goal that was never meant for us.

We want to see ourselves achieve our greatest potential across a range of circumstances. When we make sacrifices to achieve goals, develop relationships or get a job, it is often out of a sense of obligation to the social identity, a sense that we are not good enough. We strive to achieve more and more to compensate for neglecting our innermost identity. We spin on a treadmill of our own imagination, running after signposts of success. We assume that the grass is greener on the other side.

Throughout our lifetime, we have thousands of 'sliding doors' moments, or chances to alter our path, some leading us to positive outcomes and others to negative ones. Each key decision offers growth opportunities. Each sends us on a distinct path where we commit ourselves to new patterns of behaviour.

There is a great temptation to be preoccupied with regrets over past decisions. But all this is in retrospect; no one can predict the outcomes of a decision. However, we can prepare for opportunities today and draw insights from our current experiences. Revealing moments arise in different ways—people we interact with, projects at work, family issues and other unexpected turns in life. These moments give us insight into our inner needs. Thinking alone and living in the world of our mind does not lead to all the insights that we might have hoped for. It's only when we are in the midst of the decisions that we may suddenly realize: 'Oh shit, I don't like where I am.'

When that light sparks in our minds and a new path excites us, the feeling is palpable. A surge of energy floods us with a renewed sense of what we really want from life. The direction we ought to follow comes from tuning into what excites us, but we need the courage to follow that flow.

When we think about it, the feeling that we are off-track is intertwined with our self-esteem. We often face hurdles in situations or relationships. These can irritate us and even affect our sense of self-worth. These irritations are often just part of life. But they may be signs that there is another better path to take. If we look within, we may see that our decisions and actions are associated with at least some degree of self-esteem or confidence in ourselves. Even when decisions are uncertain, there may be at least some confidence that we can correct our course later as needed. However, this confidence dissipates very tangibly when we feel clearly that we are off the pathway that is right for us.

Why do we make the decisions that we later feel don't represent our most authentic pathway? One reason is that each of us has different sides to our personality, which we bring into play in varied ways in different situations. Another reason is that we feel that we have no choice but to make decisions on the basis of fear or a desire for security.

How we show up in the world today is a function of countless experiences starting in our early years of life. These experiences are interwoven with choices that we have made along the way, as well as our current pursuits and commitments. The point is that as we are carried through the stream of time, we are never the same. We are constantly adjusting and evolving. Society often tells us to measure ourselves according to external standards and milestones. But is this really necessary? What if our reliance on external goal-based standards only drags our centre of gravity downwards? What if it inspires fear-based decision-making rather than living the inspired life that we are called to live? Perhaps the truer goal is to focus on the inner journey and the deeper unfolding of the self.

## HEAD OR HEART

Frank was on the road to rising up the career ladder. He was set to take a high-paying job that involved travel, late nights and weekend work. The opportunity had all the trappings of success and offered a track to further bonuses and promotions. He put a lot of thought into this prospect. In one sense, it was the right way to go. But his heart was not in it. He felt a resistance within himself. Instead of feeling beholden to outward standards of success, he actually felt greater contentment when he considered something else—his relationship with his partner. He wanted to spend more time with him. Frank decided to choose quality time with his partner over the potential new job. His career path was not as important as his relationship. Even though his current job paid almost 30 per cent less, he had no regrets [9].

There is no substitute for contentment. Many people intuitively suspect that listening to your heart is good. 'Take a leap of faith', 'follow your intuition' and 'don't follow the status quo' are the familiar maxims for life. But following our heart is easier said than done. It requires inner strength and trust in our gut instincts. We, humans, are naturally wired to be risk-averse, so we often resort to making decisions with our heads and push our intuitions to the side.

In today's culture, using our cognitive abilities to make decisions is considered ideal. We are judged and ranked on the basis of our cognitive intelligence. When it comes to 'head versus heart', many of us will follow the head. If we think deeply, most of us know the feeling of decisions not being right. It is not based on logic, yet it fuels a sense of doubt over our choices. We are told not to trust these feelings. However, our emotions are like an internal GPS. We cannot ignore it. But when we feel this way, we may avoid facing those feelings. We stay put in the same job or relationship, for various reasons, maybe to avoid the unknown. Even though we have created outwardly successful social identities, there seems to be no satisfaction.

Alex Bratty, a research strategist and author of *Leverage the Science of Happiness to Increase Performance, Productivity, and Profitability*, offers tips on how to handle the heart versus head conundrum. She states that the three questions that we ask ourselves when we make choices are

> *What do I really want?*
> *Why do I want to do this?*
> *And how do I want to feel when I have this?*

'Put any decision through these three simple but effective questions and really listen to the answers. Allow yourself to have a balance between your emotions and your mind.'

She adds that the *why* of what we want is of greater importance.

> The motivation and intention behind our actions matter. If we act out of fear or from a place of 'should' we're usually not taking action that's aligned with who we truly are and what we really want in life. We may also find that our actions are not that productive and that we seem to be spinning our wheels rather than

actually getting somewhere or achieving something. On the other hand, when we're coming from a place of knowing and well-being, we are more likely to be in alignment with what we truly desire and that means what we do, comes from a place of inspired action. This is because we're clear on what we want and why we want it, so the action-steps to get there become obvious and have more impact in achieving our goal. [10]

A lot of thought is needed to understand what we want from life. We are told that feelings lie to us, but not all of them are baseless. If we can make decisions boldly, with introspection and understanding, we can make measured decisions. We then know what we want to prioritize in our lives so we will be able to say, 'Yes, this is what I want, I am pleased with my decisions, and I am content where I am, I have achieved my goal.'

That's the meaning of success. The reason we often choose to not engage in discovering our true potential is that we lack the self-belief to follow through. Fear makes us hold back and not move forward.

## FEAR FACTORS

Diana Malerba, life coach and neurolinguistic programming (NLP) practitioner, shares that fear can be an ally if we try to understand it better. She uses a metaphor of a tree to explain [11].

> If you consider the way fear works, you'll notice that it's an internal process. It happens in your mind, it's often generated by a thought or an image that connects to some other core fears and it impacts your whole being. Like a tree, it starts from the roots and goes up to the trunk, where it finds its strength, and it keeps going up to the branches and prevents you from moving forward.

That's when we feel stuck and unable to move. We see opportunities, but we are unable to take action. Malerba suggests an introspection.

> You can quietly observe this process inside you while it happens. You think about something, whether it's a thought or an image, and suddenly, a negative scenario comes up, it's just imagined, but you can feel the fear in your body. If you are still there and sitting quietly, you can locate that feeling inside you. It has a shape, a colour, a temperature. You can even describe the feeling of that emotion when it touches your body. So the process of scaring ourselves is an internal one. It happens in our minds, it impacts our whole being and it pushes us to react. It has concrete consequences in our lives. [12]

Malerba explains that we don't have to succumb to this debilitating feeling. 'If fear takes its power from showing you potentially dangerous consequences of your actions, you can take your power back by questioning if those consequences are real. Because if they aren't, you don't need that fear anymore.'

When fear prevents people from achieving their goals, psychologists call it self-sabotaging behaviour. The way out is to build courage and belief that one can achieve. This courage drives us towards our goals. The lessons of successful individuals tell us about the obstacles they have overcome to achieve their ambitions.

Paytm's CEO Vijay Shekhar Sharma is the son of a simple schoolteacher. He was from a small village near Aligarh that had limited internet and mobile connectivity. He wanted to develop a company that provided an Indian e-commerce payment system accessible from anywhere. Paytm is considered India's largest mobile payments and commerce platform, and it can transfer money instantly to anyone. Sharma didn't have the finances to set up his business. He had to borrow to fund his start-up.

The loan repayments were difficult. He took up a few part-time jobs to make ends meet and to help cover his debts. Despite all this, he achieved his goal. And his advice is to aim high. 'If you don't work every day to create history and change the destiny of your country, your community, or the business world, you are really wasting your time. Do not stop with anything small and that is what matters the most,' he says [13].

Many students are discouraged by the idea that business success can only be attained with financial backing and a long string of elite academic qualifications. This is not the case with many entrepreneurs, young or old, and of any gender, who have succeeded despite poverty, poor education and limited business experience.

Patricia Narayan is one such high-achieving lady. Thirty years ago, she started her career as an entrepreneur, selling eateries from a mobile cart on a beach. She was going through a personal hell: battling a failed marriage, coping with an abusive husband who was an addict and raising two young children. Patricia now owns a chain of 14 restaurants with over 200 hundred employees working for her [14].

When Usaamah Siddique took a business management course, he had no idea how much his career path was going to change. He was always creative at heart. He wanted to do something different and unique. When an opportunity came up to work with a celebrity stylist, he jumped at it. He was enamoured by the fashion world and felt that there was so much he could share about it in his own creative way. He started blogging about men's fashions. It wasn't exactly a lucrative way to make money. In fact, it was a risky venture, because with men's fashion there is limited creative freedom to make it exciting. Siddique was not deterred. He had a vision and believed that he would succeed in creating a blog that would be eye-catching and attract followers. Less than a decade later, Siddique has made his mark in the world of influencer marketing. He has created a unique presence on Instagram and is one of the country's leading fashion and travel influencers. He has his own label named after his blog—The Dapper Label—and has collaborated with popular men's clothing brands. These internationally well-reputed brands eagerly approach him to model their products. Siddique has earned a reputation for being sincere and genuine when dealing with brand names.

Siddique shares that to achieve success, the most important factor is belief in oneself. He added that we often seek approval of our peers or family, but what we really need is the approval from our inner self. 'When I started off, the digital space wasn't as vast as it is today, and what I was stepping into didn't seem like a lucrative industry. I believed in my work and I believed that someday it [would] be recognized and valued. Believing in my work and myself was the first thing I ever did' [15].

These inspiring success stories showed that belief in oneself was vital. In addition, there was no focus on outward validation or seeking approval, but rather simply a passion that drove these entrepreneurs towards their goals. They simply focused on what they wanted out of their lives and what they needed to achieve. They were mentally strong and didn't shrink in the face of failure.

Real life doesn't always offer easy choices. We may feel scattered or lost between competing options and priorities. We may carry a sense of failure and even call ourselves 'hopeless'. We compare ourselves with others who seem to have it all together, when all we want to do is surrender to our self-doubts. These kinds of feelings affect our choices every day. Psychologists have said that frustration, regret and unhealthy beliefs tend to drain our energy. But when we take responsibility and focus, we are back in control and we have the energy to make changes that are in tune with our own unique pathway.

## BEING REALISTIC

There is a natural tendency to envy others or aspire to be like them, or to think that one can handle the same responsibilities as others, but the truth is that one must realize what one is capable of.

Deepak always wanted to excel in athletics. When his colleagues went on hiking trips, wakeboarding or run marathons, he wished he could go with them. He joined them on some outdoor activities but in time he realized he didn't like it at all. Slowly, Deepak realized that even though he tried, he had to confront the fact that he wasn't athletic. He accepted this reality and chose not to compare and compete.

Being realistic and accepting of one's limitations is part of knowing oneself. As we grow older and interact with the world, we discover more about our capabilities and weaknesses. This is the route to greater fulfilment. A lack of understanding of ourselves and our skills, or even our likes or dislikes, will lead to detours and poorly chosen goals. By contrast, if we have clear self-knowledge, we will be able to make better life choices that are suited to our personality.

The philosopher Socrates famously declared that an unexamined life was not worth living. Although the statement may seem stark, the broader point is useful. Asked to sum up what all the philosophical rules could be reduced to, he offered, 'know yourself.'

Self-knowledge is not possible in isolation. It is hard-won through experiences in our jobs and interacting with others. We need to test our abilities and see where we fail and where we thrive. As we experience the ongoing stream of opportunities and challenges, these insights guide us forward.

## BOTTOM LINE

Thriving in the world requires making a commitment to self-knowledge. This skill develops not just from experience but also from observing ourselves dispassionately without judgement, just as we might observe nature. The greater our self-knowledge, the more we can fully appreciate our true value and contribute appropriately to the world.

Each of us is influenced by distinct families and cultural settings. As a result, no two people manifest the same talents. Remembering this can help us to appreciate and embrace those around us. Recognizing our human dignity, and that of others, is an essential foundation for wellness and a sense of community.

We need to understand which of our impulses and dreams stem from our fear-based mind and which stem from our evolved mind. When emotional pain is triggered in us, our inner wisdom and other strengths can be blocked. When we simmer inside, we lack the focus needed to serve others well. Being mentally robust requires commitment and regular practice.

Be prepared to declare your independence from the dynamics of a culture that does not support your wellness and that of others. As Mitch Albom says in his book, *Tuesdays with Morrie*, 'the culture we have does not make people feel good about ourselves. And you have to be strong enough to say if the culture doesn't work, don't buy it.'

Possessed of internal strength, we can then confront our fears and challenges, leading to the foundation of our inner balance.

## REFERENCES

1. Williams E. 2017. How much do you think you are worth? This story might open your eyes. Curious Mind Magazine; 2017. Available at https://

curiousmindmagazine.com/much-think-worth/ (accessed on 19 January 2021).
2. HumanMetrics. Personality type explained; 2019. Available at http://www.humanmetrics.com/personality/type (accessed on 19 January 2021).
3. Schmidt M. Finding and letting go of the self through the enneagram and spiritual practices. Social Conscience and Inner Awakening; 2016. Available at https://martinschmidtinasia.wordpress.com/2016/12/21/purifying-your-purpose-finding-and-letting-go-of-yourself-in-service-society-and-the-sacred/ (accessed on 19 January 2021).
4. Brooks D. Opinion | The moral bucket list. The New York Times; 2015. Available at https://www.nytimes.com/2015/04/12/opinion/sunday/david-brooks-the-moral-bucket-list.html (accessed on 19 January 2021).
5. Kendra C. Erik Erikson's stages of psychosocial development. Verywellmind; 2020. Available at https://www.verywellmind.com/erik-eriksons-stages-of-psychosocial-development–2795740 (accessed on 19 January 2021).
6. Leena. E-mail interview. London; 2020.
7. Cherry, Kendra. How our identity forms out of conflict; 2019 https://www.verywellmind.com/what-is-an-identity-crisis-2795948 (accessed on 23 Feb 2021).
8. DSDWEB. Explain how individual identity and self-esteem are linked to emotional and spiritual wellbeing; 2019. Available at https://dsdweb.co.uk/level–2-diploma-in-care/implement-person-centred-approaches-in-care-settings/explain-how-individual-identity-and-self-esteem-are-linked-to-emotional-and-spiritual-wellbeing/ (accessed on 19 January 2021).

9. Frank. Phone chat. London; 2020.
10. Bratty A. Decision making—Head vs heart vs gut; 2015. Available at https://www.alexbratty.com/decision-making-head-vs-heart-vs-gut/ (accessed on 19 January 2021).
11. Malerba D. How to gain confidence and courage/01. The Brave Hearted; 2016. Available at http://www.thebravehearted.ch/your-fear-is-a-tree-01/ (accessed on 19 January 2021).
12. Malerba D. How to gain confidence and courage/02. The Brave Hearted; n.d. Available at http://www.thebravehearted.ch/your-fear-is-a-tree-01/ (accessed on 19 January 2021).
13. Padhiar J. 10 successful entrepreneurs in India who you should follow right away. *MYHQ Digest*; 2019. Available at https://digest.myhq.in/successful-entrepreneurs-in-india/ (accessed on 19 January 2021).
14. BizEncyclopedia. An empowering tale of perseverance and survival: the success story of Patricia Narayan; n.d. Available at https://www.bizencyclopedia.com/article/an-empowering-tale-of-perseverance-and-survival-the-success-story-of-patricia-narayan (accessed on 16 November 2020).
15. Siddique U. WhatsApp interview by author; Mumbai; 2020.

# CHAPTER 9

# AWARENESS THROUGH SELF-COMPASSION

*When you love yourself, there's a lightness to your being. That self-love, that lightness, that sense of humour, that is what being spiritual is about, and that is the state of consciousness that really opens you up to your intuition and to your guidance from the other side.*

—Anita Moorjani

Losing self-worth is a powerful curse. It is said that in the Solomon Islands, in the South Pacific Sea, when the inhabitants want to fell a large tree, they gather around it in a large group. Then they start cursing and yelling at the tree. This is repeated often and after a month the tree withers and dies. The story seems amazing, but it is powerful as a metaphor.

This is what happens to people when they are made to feel inferior. They believe they are useless and have no value or place in this world. Without self-worth, a person suffers deep hurt. This often stems from incidents in childhood. Once an unhealthy belief is formed, the child internalizes this way of thinking.

Mumbai-based Counselling Psychologist Sanam Devidasani says that how we are conditioned in our formative years affects how we view the world: 'Automatic thoughts are governed by one's core beliefs. These are the fundamental and deep-rooted beliefs that a person develops since childhood about the world, others and themselves. These beliefs are our absolute truths. Once these beliefs are formed, they are reluctant to change. So we do everything in our power to view the world through the lens of those beliefs and twist events in our lives to fit that belief.'

Our emotional pain doesn't just disappear. The way we feel can distort our ability to adapt, and we can find ways to avoid that pain. Devidasani says:

> People with low self-esteem often have a lot of fears. Fear of saying something stupid, fear of being boring, fear of losing people, fear of meeting new people, fear of trying new things, fear of hurting someone and so on. The most common escape for fear is avoidance. If you are afraid of meeting someone new, you make an excuse and cancel your plan. If you are afraid of giving a presentation at work, you call in sick and avoid the presentation. Avoidance does temporarily bring down your anxiety, but it also reinforces the thought that there is something to fear [1].

## KILLERS OF SELF-WORTH

Dr Gabor Maté specializes in the study and treatment of addiction and trauma. Maté is quoted as saying that, to avoid emotional pain, almost everyone has some kind of an addiction. This addiction may not be to drugs but to anything that gives them relief, be it food, social media scrolling, video games, sex, work or even shopping. Maté says that addictions to any of these tap into the same brain circuits that drug use activates.

Maté also believes that the root cause of addictive behaviours can be linked to distressing experiences in childhood. Maté points out that when a person has experienced psychological trauma, the psyche becomes harder and less flexible. Using a metaphor to explain the emotional effect, he points out that when we are physically wounded and healed, scar tissue forms which is harder and less flexible than the tissue that it replaces. Similarly, when we have suffered emotional pain, which is scar tissue of the mind, addictions become an easier way to numb the suffering rather than change the way we think. He explains that emotional pain and shame is at the heart of addiction. It is avoidance of reality that results in so much more harm [2].

A young woman spent most of her formative years avoiding pain. Her story gives us insight into the ways unhealthy beliefs and emotional pain can lead to addiction.

Hong Kong-based Indian, 30-year-old Mehek Gidwani is a Kundalini Meditation Teacher and an Addiction Recovery Coach. To become the healthy balanced person she is today, Gidwani went through very troubled times. It started when she was in primary school. She was generally a shy child and didn't have a voice to stand up for herself. She was the youngest of three daughters and mostly kept to herself. She studied at an international school, where the children were predominantly Chinese. Gidwani found it difficult to make friends because the children avoided her. She was regarded as dirty or smelly, called 'hairy yeti' because of the colour of her skin. She recalls distinctly: 'In Primary 1, no one would hold my hand, when we lined up to go to class. It destroyed me and I took it to heart.'

Gidwani didn't tell anyone about the nasty words and bullying that went on for years. She suffered quietly and internalized that there was something wrong with her. She never told her parents about how much she hated school, and often she would feign illness just so she could stay at home. After a few years, she found a group of friends and her school life improved significantly. Still, she was often made fun of and hence she was resultantly insecure. In Primary 6, before she moved to secondary school, she vowed she would not be bullied anymore.

As a teenager, Gidwani made an effort to adjust to her new school environment. She even socialized more trying to fit into a group. Gidwani would often go to the mall on Saturday afternoons. One Saturday, Gidwani went to the mall with a group of older youngsters. They spent majority of the afternoon in the smoking area outside the mall. A few of them were sitting in a stairwell. Gidwani, fearful to join them, stayed outside. Eventually, she got restless and mustered up enough courage to chat with them. As she entered the stairwell, one of them suddenly grabbed her and pulled his sleeve over her face. Next thing she felt was a sense of intoxication. She heard bells and her vision altered as if she was looking through a fish-eye camera lens. She experienced a three-minute high. It was the first time she had inhaled a muscle relaxant spray. She was disoriented, and one of them helped her sit down while she went through a very unusual experience that made her numb and brought a sense of wonder and excitement. The group kind of cheered for her and laughed with her. Gidwani felt a sense of acceptance, a feeling she had missed as a child.

Gidwani began to socialize more with this group. Over the next year, inhaling muscle relaxant became a weekly activity. From the age of 15, but from this point on, her descent into substance use was hard to resist. For the next few years, Gidwani continued to substance abuse: muscle relaxants for about two years, later it was ketamine for almost three years and she smoked marijuana for about five years. The drugs gave her a feeling of relaxation and she felt socially comfortable.

## Chapter 9: Awareness through Self-compassion

Her anxieties faded away. Her inner critic was silenced. Feelings were numbed. When she turned 17, her grades dropped and she was badly affected by her addiction. Her eyes were bloodshot, her eating habits were erratic and even though she thought she was in control, she was smoking marijuana constantly. Even at home and in her room, she was unable to stop the urge to take a puff.

Around that time, Gidwani began to realize the truth about her sexuality. She was attracted to her girlfriend, a feeling she tried to avoid. Her infatuation for a guy was, in retrospect, manufactured. Gidwani was confused and resisted how she felt. 'I didn't want it to be true and was scared of what others would think of me.' When Gidwani's friends discovered that she was gay, they made fun of her.

Feelings of isolation closed in on her. 'Even in a room full of people, I felt an intense sense of loneliness, and my ability to connect with others was vastly compromised. I struggled to explain myself in a way that people would understand, and I even struggled to hold a conversation. My mind was so scattered that I would lose focus in the conversation. My mind was filled with the mistruths and delusions of reality. Like most human beings, I made up stories and considered them as truth. Stories of why that person didn't like me, why the girl I liked was avoiding me, why my family didn't understand me. When someone pointed out the holes in my stories, I would get very defensive. I distanced myself from those around me. Many people thought I was insane. Because of my erratic behaviour, many people distanced themselves from me. I felt alone. My addiction secluded me. I felt an enormous sense of loneliness, the most I've ever felt.'

She continued to numb her pain with drugs and alcohol. Her mother eventually found out. When her mother confronted her, Gidwani was defensive, saying she wasn't addicted. 'In that moment of false courage, I told her I was gay.'

Saying it out loud confirmed the truth of her reality. It was difficult to accept, but she knew deep down in her heart that she had to face it. Gidwani's mother responded emotionally, 'Why are you doing this to me?'

Gidwani's family didn't believe that she was really gay. They assumed that she was making it all up. They were more concerned about her addiction. 'They tried to tell me that I was not in control and I should get help. My thinking was that they didn't understand.'

Around that time, Gidwani was accepted into a UK University. This was an opportunity to prove that she was an independent woman in control of her life. Gidwani left for the UK, but things didn't turn out as she had hoped.

Gidwani was emotionally weak and her self-esteem was rock bottom. She was still abusing drugs and alcohol; they caused paranoia, delusion and perpetuated poor mental health. She was ashamed of her inability to stop her urges. She failed miserably that year in the university. It was an eye-opener and Gidwani realized she did need help. Eventually, she was taken to rehab by her family. She no longer had the will to resist. For so long she had numbed her feelings, but now she would have to face them. It was going to require strength and conviction.

'Rehab was the best thing that ever happened to me,' Gidwani said. She was 19 years old at that time and there were a lot of suppressed feelings and emotional pain to address. After almost eight months of counselling, group therapy, yoga, equine, art and other therapies, she was able to heal. It took tremendous amount of self-acceptance to get on the path of recovery.

'My journey was of self-exploration. It was an inner journey to understand that my addiction was rooted in avoidance of pain. My depression came from the suppression of emotions. My self-love was destroyed while I was in school. And I was ashamed of who I really was.'

After rehab, Gidwani moved into a small apartment and returned to the university. She continued to attend group therapy while she avidly followed the 12-step-recovery programme, a model used by Narcotics Anonymous and Alcoholics Anonymous. She attended their meetings regularly. She remained committed to her goal of staying sober and has succeeded since then. After three years, she graduated first-class honours in industrial product design.

Gidwani's journey to recovery wasn't just about staying clean; it was also about changing her ways of thinking and developing mental strength. To understand and accept the world as it is, Gidwani discovered new mental processes to deal with life and not let it affect her mindset. Even now, she constantly monitors her thoughts. 'I have learned to take inventory of what I am good at or bad at. Humility is having a balanced perspective of oneself, which means I am not shit nor am I perfect, and I accept myself the way I am. When I get hurt, I face the pain and understand why I am feeling this way.'

How does she deal with critical remarks?

> When someone says something hurtful, I try to understand why they said what they did, but I practise not sinking into self-loathing. I keep my focus on validating myself. I search for the truth in the statement and practise accepting any truthful aspects of it. It doesn't mean I am bad, but maybe there's something I need to change about myself. If the statement is made out of bias, I let it go. From my experiences of being bullied at school and not feeling accepted; I grew up with the belief that I wasn't good enough. Many people have this subconscious belief about themselves. I rewire this thinking by repeating to myself that 'I am inherently good enough.'

She rediscovered her relationship with her body, her sexuality, her self-esteem and herself.

> I now understand that the external world cannot validate me. I have to understand that I wasn't bullied because there is

something wrong with me. Some children are not actively taught. They learn through observation to discriminate and look down on other people. It is not their fault that they grew up with those kinds of beliefs. We meet a diverse number of people with differing perceptions, and we don't all view the world in the same way. We live in a connected world that tells us how we should dress or behave or be a certain way to be accepted. We don't have to fit into those norms. It's easy to believe that we're not good enough if we don't fit into our culture's definition of success, beauty or prosperity.

She says that when she is hurt, her subconscious response is to rely on protection mechanisms, such as arrogance, self-righteousness or defensiveness. At other times, she deeply criticizes herself. 'I need to accept my limitations and those of others and not diminish myself in the process.'

What about her mother's response? 'My mum's perception has changed; she accepts me for who I am and the way I am. She is my cheerleader now. She invited me to a Diwali luncheon in one of her Indian ladies' group. I dressed as I pleased, in a shirt and pair of trousers. My mum proudly introduced me to her friends. It was a wonderful feeling to be accepted.'

To maintain inner balance, Gidwani says, 'It is important for me to understand my own frailties, and then I can understand others. I can help others because I know what it feels like to be bullied, to be ashamed, to be alone, to feel like I don't fit in. I practise changing myself and accepting my limitations without judgement. We are all connected, and we all share the common human experience. Pain is not permanent; it comes to teach us something better and to help others to deal with their pain.'

Gidwani suggests, 'keep saying "I am inherently worthy" when facing a self-hate moment.'

Gidwani is now a strong and confident young woman. She has courageously faced her life experiences and is on a journey of helping others to understand that they are not alone when they suffer. The important fact is that Gidwani had moments when she could have given in to defeat, but she never gave up and courageously chose to follow the path of recovery. Gidwani says that faith, surrendering her will to God and support from her friends and family, all helped her recover a healthy mindset [3].

'Not all addictions are rooted in abuse or trauma, but I do believe they can all be traced to painful experiences,' Dr Gabor Maté writes in his bestseller, *In the Realm of Hungry Ghosts: Close Encounters with Addiction* [4].

> A hurt is at the centre of all addictive behaviours. It is present in the gambler, the Internet addict, the compulsive shopper, and the workaholic. The wound may not be as deep and the ache not as excruciating, and it may even be entirely hidden—but it's there.

## SELF FIRST, THEN OTHERS

Shveitta Sethi Sharma is an expert on interpersonal relationships and has been credited with the gift of being able to help people feel good about themselves. She has shared her views on TEDxHKUST and is inspired to create a billion happy faces. Her philosophy is that we must be happy with ourselves first. 'I remember during my Cathay Pacific inflight service training days, our instructor told us that during a decompression when oxygen masks are deployed, the first thing to do is to place it on yourself and then help others.'

She added that passengers with children are also advised to put their masks first. 'If you are incapacitated, you are in no position to help others, so the first thing to do is to look after yourself and then look after those around you.'

Sharma suggests having the same philosophy in our daily life. 'These days, there is so much talk about practising empathy, kindness and compassion but, in this cacophony, we forget that the first person who needs our kindness and compassion is ourselves. In our desire to please everyone around us, we sometimes forget that we owe ourselves the love and compassion that is expected of us. Just as an incapacitated passenger is of no help to others, we too cannot give what we don't have.'

She explains that it is not our fault that we have become insecure and fearful. Everywhere we turn, we are manipulated into thinking that we are not good enough. We are constantly being reminded of our lack. 'We give away our personal power to outsiders who gain from our insecurities. The marketers sell us stuff by using our insecurities as the building blocks of their products.'

Sharma points out that we need to accept ourselves the way we are and practise self-compassion. We need to understand that we are good enough and just as everyone around us deserves love and empathy, so do we. 'Practicing self-acceptance is the first step towards healing and growth. Once you accept yourself completely you give yourself the permission to start healing.'

Sharma says that her goal is straightforward: to be happy and help others to find what makes them happy. It sounds deceptively simple yet very hard to achieve because of layers of conditioning from childhood. Finding ways to tap into ourselves and our needs helps us to discover which actions inspire and which ones create anxiety [5].

Marcus Buckingham, author of *Now, Discover Your Strengths*, explains that 'Strengths are the things you do to energise you; your weaknesses are the things you do to deplete you.' More than focusing on your weaknesses, he suggests discovering what makes you brilliant. He defines strength not as something that you are good at but as an activity that motivates you and makes you feel energized.

> A strength is more appetite than ability, and it's that appetite that drives us to want to do it again; practice more; refine it to perfection. The appetite leads to the practice, which leads to performance. Leveraging your strengths and managing around your weaknesses isn't just about making yourself feel better. It's about conditioning yourself to contribute the best of yourself, every day. It's about performance.[6]

Moving towards a goal that makes us strong is far better than being moved by fear. Our motivations should be clear in our minds. We are not going towards a goal out of external pressure or societal expectations, but purely by what we choose to do [7].

Devidasani is a strong believer in looking inwards to ensure well-being rather than depending on changing external factors. 'When I see clients, they talk a lot about how external factors such as people, work, city and media are eliciting negative emotions in them and how they'd like the people or situations to change or disappear. I ask them, 'If there's a room filled with 100 people, will they all react in the same way as you are in this situation?' The answer is always no. That is because everyone perceives situations, people and circumstances in a different way. This perception of a situation, and your thoughts about it, is what influences how you feel about that situation. This self-work is the way to well-being rather than changing the people or anything else that is external in your life.'

## SELF-ESTEEM THIEVES

Reema Khanna is a Hong Kong-based psychologist. She says that 'If you constantly feel "I am a loser" or "I should be ashamed" or "I am worthless" or "I am a misfit"; these negative thoughts will affect the choices you make and how you act. I call all these sentences the self-esteem thieves!'

Khanna shared that Abraham Maslow, a leading theorist in self-esteem, believed that human behaviours are driven by needs such as personal importance, social acceptance and being valued.

'The growth of self-esteem ultimately leads to what Maslow refers to as self-actualization. Self-actualization is not a stagnant point. It is an ongoing process when a person feels that they have achieved well-being, fulfilment and personal creativity. Thus, self-esteem and self-fulfilment work side by side. Via self-esteem, a person can feel that they can achieve self-fulfilment' [8].

When you talk to yourself in a kind, non-judgemental way—the same way you would encourage a loved one, you feel motivated rather than stuck with your critical voice. Research shows that self-compassion can motivate people to improve their mistakes, failures or shortcomings because they view them more objectively.

Kristin Neff, PhD, is an associate professor of educational psychology at the University of Texas at Austin. Neff is considered the pioneer of the idea of self-compassion as a tool to help people with low self-esteem. She explains that compassion towards the self is the quickest route to raising self-esteem.

In one of Neff's academic papers, she shares the disadvantages of social comparisons. In a story, she takes the example of a singer–songwriter who is performing for the first time at a local coffee house. After the performance, the singer asks for feedback and receives a comment, 'average'. How would the singer feel? Ashamed or embarrassed? Feel like a failure? Neff comments that in our incredibly competitive society, being 'average' is not good enough. We have to be above average to be worthy of other people's opinion.

The trouble is that it is impossible for anyone to be above average all the time [9].

Kristin Neff, along with Christopher Germer, PhD, who is also an expert on self-compassion, have shared interesting insights in their book, *The Mindful Self-compassion Workbook: A Proven Way to Accept Yourself, Build Inner Strength, and Thrive*. They explain that many people assume that self-compassion is a form of self-pity. But, in fact, it is a remedy. Self-pity is a weakness. While self-pity says 'poor me', self-compassion recognizes that life is hard for everyone and therefore one needs to find a way to make do. Compassionate people are more capable of considering different perspectives rather than wallowing in feelings of despair. They don't dwell unduly on the worst parts of life. They try to make the best of a difficult situation.

The authors further explain that when we activate the reptilian brain, through self-criticism, we tend to react as if there is a hostile external environment when, in fact, we are attacking ourselves. These feelings can result in stress and anxiety leading to depression. 'When the stress response (fight–flight–freeze) is triggered by a threat to our self-concept, we are likely to turn on ourselves in an unholy trinity of reactions. We fight ourselves (self-criticism), we flee from others (isolation), or we freeze (rumination).'

'Compassion, including self-compassion, is linked to the mammalian care system. That's why being compassionate to ourselves when we feel inadequate makes us feel safe and cared for, like a child held in a warm embrace.' Neff and Germer share that self-compassionate people not only have greater self-confidence but are less likely to fear failure and are more likely to try again when they fail and to persist in learning [10].

Neff suggests that the three components of self-compassion are self-kindness, common humanity and mindfulness [11].

- Self-kindness enables us to comfort ourselves as one would comfort a friend. Instead of berating ourselves or feeling anger towards our mistakes, we show care and concern.
- Common humanity means that we are imperfect human beings, and we all experience some form of pain. Suffering is common to all of mankind. We accept the reality that there will be some ups and downs. Saying 'why me?' only makes the pain worse.
- Mindfulness helps us to be aware of our negative thoughts. Compassion flows in when we accept the fact that there is pain and suffering. We don't create an identity of negativity but one that is balanced and peaceful.

Self-compassion is not about self-evaluation; it is about being kind to oneself. And where better to develop this thought process than in schools? Cultivating compassion in children has helped, in some cases, to reduce bullying and aggressive behaviour.

Marty Schmidt has been a humanities teacher at the Hong Kong International School for 30 years and is the author of *Wisdom Way of Teaching: Educating for Social Conscience and Inner Awakening in the High School Classroom*. He shares how he teaches self-love [12].

> In order to cultivate this kind of compassion on a daily basis, many students find the *loving kindness* meditation very effective, which starts with care for the self, and then moves to progressively caring for others. In this sense, attention is paid to the self but not to the obsessive 'woe-is-me' mindset that often accompanies low self-esteem. Thus, in my teaching experience, the best antidote for such issues is actually empathetically joining students to the rest of humanity through service and mindfulness practices.

Studies have shown that if one is to take the angle of self-esteem, a spiral of thoughts which can complicate the growth process, but with self-compassion, self-esteem doesn't get knocked down. With self-compassion, we can better understand that our mistakes do not automatically make us a bad person. Instead, we recognize that our worth is unconditional. Research has consistently shown a positive link between self-compassion and overall well-being, which provides a sense of self-worth in a way that is not narcissistic.

Dr Allen Dorcas, Counselling Psychologist and Senior Teaching Fellow at the Hong Kong Polytechnic University, says,

> ...low self-esteem is incompatible with self-compassion. If we don't like ourselves, have a lot of inner self-judgements about ourselves (could range from appearance, personality, culture, background and so on), we are not able to be open and caring towards ourselves. Self-compassion points at an ability to embrace oneself, to accept who we are as we are and to be gentle and loving towards oneself. The more we can grow in our ability to do this, the more naturally our level of self-acceptance leads to higher self-esteem. I can then honestly say I am ok being who I am, and I can even like who I am. Consequently, self-doubt and self-judgement will decrease [13].

## BE WATER: FLOW, RESILIENCE AND SELF-ESTEEM

Bruce Lee, best known for being a martial artist and action film star, was a deeply introspective man. His daughter, Shannon Lee, believes that her father was one of the most notable and profound philosophers of the 20th century. She wrote a book, *Be Water, My Friend*, where she explains one of his more popular philosophies, 'the idea of being like water is to attempt to embody the qualities of fluidity and naturalness in one's life. Water can adjust its shape to any container, it can be soft or strong, it is simply and naturally always itself, and it finds a way to keep moving and flowing'.

Bruce Lee was named one of *Time* magazine's 100 Greatest Men of the Century. He blended Eastern and Western thoughts into a personal philosophy of self-development. He stated, 'In order to control myself I must first accept myself by going with and not against my nature' [14].

If going with our nature is a way to flow with ease, we don't fight or criticize ourselves. In Taoism, flow is referred to as Wu Wei which in Chinese means doing nothing. It is not about being lazy but about being so immersed in action that it becomes an 'effortless doing'. It also means being able to carry out an activity with inner calm despite a frenetic environment. Hungarian-American Psychologist Mihaly Csikszentmihalyi spoke of something similar, absorption in an activity where nothing else mattered, which he called flow [15]. During his research in the 1980s and 1990s, he was intrigued by artists who would forget themselves while they were immersed in their activity. They were not worried about the failure or judgement of others. They were totally consumed in their work.

In recent years, flow ideas have been applied in business, with many companies making them a core part of their philosophy. Interestingly, flow and resilience are related. They reflect our self-discipline, our commitment to an activity. Resilience is an ability that enables us to adapt and rediscover ways to remain in control, yet be fluid in our intentions towards the tasks at hand. It is a skill that can be acquired through practice.

In life, we face inevitable uncertainty. When we are resilient, we bounce back in the face of adversity. We handle problems without falling apart. We are mindful but do not lose hope. Instead, we take on any obstacle as a way to learn and grow. These experiences lead to courage that helps us to achieve our greatest potential without being burdened by external validation.

Clinical Psychologist Dr Guy Winch calls self-esteem our 'emotional immune system'. In a podcast transcript, he describes self-esteem saying:

> It's like the armour that we wear to the battle of life. We want to strengthen that armour, and I really would urge people to think of their self-esteem like body armour that they wear to life. You would never want to poke holes in that armour, so whenever you have this internal dialogue in your head that's negative and self-deprecating and self-critical and self-blaming, realize you are poking holes in your armour. [16]

## FAILING IS NOT FINAL

Creative people have been reported to have struggled with feeling incompetent or inadequate. Even though they are recognized for their talents and may even be famous, they may still have a low self-esteem. When watching their films, the actors report feeling uncomfortable, preferring not to see themselves in close-ups on 20-feet-high theatre screens, where it becomes hard not to scrutinize their appearance and performance. Because of their celebrity status, they are constantly exposed. Insecurities that arise can at times become acute.

Chirag Bajaj is an actor and a film producer based in India. 'Being in this profession, there have been situations where my self-esteem has been affected. Rejections are part of an actor's life, but still it gets to you even more when you don't know the reason for it. That's when I have negative thoughts about myself, self-doubt grows, which is then followed by regret, guilt—all of that comes into play. The most predominant thought that comes to mind most of the time is that I am probably not good enough.'

During those moments of feeling lost and confused, Bajaj made some bad choices. 'I've made impulsive decisions which backfired on me and didn't work well, which I then realized later. So having a healthy self-esteem, I feel, does play a major role in my life.'

So how does Bajaj get through self-doubts?

'I tell myself that if I wasn't good enough, how would have I gotten this far? How would it have been possible for me to make it to where I am today? Filling myself with positive thoughts and not discounting all that I have achieved helps me to keep going. It gives me the confidence I need and it doesn't let me get into a negative mind space, filled with self-doubt, which would eventually affect my self-esteem leading me further down the rabbit hole of bad decisions and unhappiness.'

Bajaj believes that self-esteem has a huge impact on mental health. 'If you are in the right state of mind, thinking clearly, staying optimistic, being nice to yourself, feeling confident about your abilities, it gives you the boost you want and makes you look at life with a positive mindset.'

He maintains his inner strength by choosing to be mindful of choices and making decisions that resonate from within. For him, the priority is finding joy from his work. 'However, I do know that, in today's day and age, being practical and using your head to make decisions is probably a better thing to do. But who can guarantee success or progress with that approach?'

He adds that failing is not final, so one must get up and try again. This is part of what makes us stronger and is part of how we learn. 'Giving yourself the permission to make mistakes is important to make progress. Learning about our strengths and weaknesses is an important part of our lives. Nobody is perfect, and I take pride in my imperfections because I know I'll only become better as I experience life.' Bajaj advocates being compassionate to yourself, especially during hardships. This and drawing on the support of your network. 'When everything around you is crumbling, that one ray of hope can very easily be yourself rather than expecting it from something or someone else. The only person you can rely on is yourself. Not to say that you shouldn't get help. Your social support also makes a lot of difference to your self-esteem. Surrounding yourself with people who uplift you rather than bogging you down is a plus.' Thus, relying on yourself as the ultimate fallback is critical. But this does not mean excluding or ignoring people around us [17].

## BOUNDARIES MATTER

Making sure that our social supports are positive is also an essential ingredient. This doesn't always come easily. We are not always able to choose who we have in our lives. Difficult bosses or colleagues and strained family relationships can eat away at our sense of self. That is where boundaries are relevant for healthy self-esteem.

Diana Malerba, a confidence coach, says that learning to set boundaries is part of learning to value yourself. It enables us to stay strong and to recognize our own needs. When we don't do that, others receive the wrong message on how to treat us. 'This is especially dangerous if you are a generous person with a tendency to give. Because you may meet people that are takers and if you don't set the limits—and make sure they are respected—you may involuntarily open the door to all sorts of abuse' [18].

We may feel that other people's expectations matter more than our own but, taken too far, this is a recipe for bad choices. It doesn't mean ignoring constructive feedback, but we must practise careful discernment, keeping in mind our vision of life. Our personal goals, talents, individuality and uniqueness matter; maintaining them is an expression of healthy self-esteem [18].

There is no quick fix to a healthy self-esteem. Living into a deeper understanding of this comes over time. We know that a tiny incident can shatter our self-esteem. And yet we know that mindful thoughts and reactions are a way to reverse the course of negative self-talk. These challenges are universal, even if the path for each of us is unique.

## CHOOSE FROM WITHIN

When Gerald went up on the stage to give his first-ever speech, he stuttered and ended up losing confidence. The audience laughed at him, and he felt deeply embarrassed. It happened in school. Thirty years later, Gerald still carries the memory of the shame and he cringes at the thought of it. He has been struggling with it ever since. He still breaks into a cold sweat every time he has to face a group of people. Gerald is in the marketing field, so he has to give sales pitches fairly often. In the back of his mind, the dread still lingers. But, fed up with this painful baggage, Gerald decided to take the bull by the horns. He chose to directly confront these memories and feelings. He won because instead of it controlling him, in the end, he became indifferent and simply dismissed it with a shrug. Gerald said, 'Yes, that was so embarrassing, how could I be so bad? How could I be so weak?' But then he added, 'So what? Hundreds of people have embarrassed themselves. I am not the only one who has been through this' [19].

Jia Jiang came to the USA with the dream of being the next Bill Gates. But despite early success in the corporate world, his first attempt to pursue his entrepreneurial dream ended in rejection. Jiang was crushed. He spiralled into deep self-doubt. But he realized that his fear of rejection was a bigger obstacle than any single rejection would ever be.

In Jia Jiang's inspiring book, *Rejection Proof: How I Beat Fear and Became Invincible Through 100 Days of Rejection*, he points out that by cowering from rejection, we reject ourselves. We miss out on experiences with no one to blame but ourselves. 'If you decide not to act out of fear of rejection, then you never get the chance to see how things could've turned out' [20].

We are afraid to face the difficult emotions that will probably never arise. We then choose to avoid the challenges or to take certain risks in case there is shame or embarrassment. We then deny ourselves because of the fear of being ridiculed.

Melissa Dahl, author of *Cringeworthy: A Theory of Awkwardness*, says that 'the moments that make us cringe are when we're yanked out of our perspective, and we can suddenly see ourselves from somebody else's point of view.'

Dahl points out that it is not merely self-compassion but self-indifference that will help us to overcome our feelings of shame. She explains that self-indifference and self-compassion are just fresh terms for an old concept: humility. Both are same in that one's own experience is part of the common human experience.

Dahl suggests that 'maybe the most compassionate attitude you can take toward yourself is to stop obsessing over yourself. Humble people don't focus on their flaws. It's more that humble people don't focus on themselves very much at all' [21].

## BOTTOM LINE

All of us hope to grow and develop. But we should compassionately recognize our natural human limits. 'We have far less control over our own behaviour than we like to think,' notes social scientist Joseph Grenny, co-author of *Change Anything: The New Science of Personal Success*.

Self-esteem, self-understanding, mindfulness and positivity are all useful for living a fulfilling life. These tools give us a chance to heal and achieve our greatest potential. Still, we have to accept that at times we will be negative and self-critical. This will be frustrating, but we should not be surprised. When our strengths seem to fail us, we can take solace from self-acceptance, which is a good thing.

This brings up a broader question: why do we try to fight our natural wiring, our natural inclinations? Our human brains are among the most complex organs to ever evolve. It is strangely ironic that we try to use our intelligence against our own nature.

This is not to say that we should let our most primitive instincts or impulses run the show. We just need not invoke our most logical, critical-thinking brain regions all the time. We have the ability to be creative, logical, empathetic, emotional, strategic, focused, imaginative and analytical. And each of us uses these qualities in varied ways. We are not fundamentally flawed; we don't need to be constantly in a fix-it mode. Our imperfect qualities are what make us human and distinct.

Rather than demanding that we always be at 100 per cent, the best thing we can do is to embrace our fluid nature. There is no use in harshly berating ourselves for falling short of a target.

And even this fluid ideal, this version of our so-called 'best' is something that can be questioned in a generous spirit of letting go. Is any single way equally the 'best' for everyone?

## REFERENCES

1. Devidasani S. E-mail interview; Mumbai; 2020.
2. Be Here Now Network. Understanding trauma, addiction, and the path to healing: A conversation with Gabor Maté; 2019. Available from: https://beherenow network.com/understanding-trauma-addiction-and-the-path-to-healing-a-conversation-with-gabor-mate/
3. Gidwani M. Face-to-face interview. Hong Kong; 2020.

4. Maté G. In the realm of hungry ghosts: close encounters with addiction. 2009. Available from: https://drgabormate.com/book/in-the-realm-of-hungry-ghosts/
5. Sharma SS. Phone chat interview. Hong Kong; 2020.
6. The Joy of Leadership (Blog). Awesome/joy/leadership; 2019. Available from: https://thejoyofleadership.home.blog/2019/11/29/the-why-behind-the-what/
7. Buckingham M. Invest in your strengths; 2018. Available from: https://www.marcusbuckingham.com/invest-in-your-strengths-2/
8. Khanna R. E-mail interview. Hong Kong; 2020.
9. Neff K. Self-compassion, self-esteem, and well-being. Soc. Personal. Psychol. Compass. 2011;5(1):1–12. Available from: https://self-compassion.org/wp-content/uploads/2015/12/SC.SE_.Well-being.pdf
10. Neff K, Germer C. The transformative effects of mindful self-compassion. Mindful; 2019. Available from: https://www.mindful.org/the-transformative-effects-of-mindful-self-compassion/
11. Neff K. Definition of self-compassion. Self-Compassion; n.d. Available from: https://self-compassion.org/the-three-elements-of-self-compassion-2/
12. Schmidt M. Phone interview. Hong Kong; 2020.
13. Dorcas A. E-mail interview. Hong Kong; 2020.
14. Popova M. Be like water: the philosophy and origin of Bruce Lee's famous metaphor for resilience. Brain Pickings; 2013. Available from: https://www.brainpickings.org/2013/05/29/like-water-bruce-lee-artist-of-life/
15. Coleman A. Zen and the art of running a business. iwoca; 2019. Available from: https://www.iwoca.co.uk/insights/the-philosophy-of-flow/

16. Gilmartin P. Mini episode: low self-esteem w/Dr. Guy Winch (voted #4 ep of 2014); 2014. Available from: https://mentalpod.com/Low-Self-Esteem-podcast
17. Bajaj C. E-mail interview. Mumbai; 2020.
18. Malerba D. How to set healthy boundaries: in 4 steps. The Brave Hearted; 2015. Available from: http://www.thebravehearted.ch/how-to-set-healthy-boundaries/
19. Gerald. Phone interview. Hong Kong; 2020.
20. Levin M. 5 lessons learned from 100 days of rejection. Inc.; 2017. Available from: https://www.inc.com/marissa-levin/5-lessons-learned-from–100-days-of-rejection.html
21. Andrew S. How to deal with cringe: a short guide to the pain pf social rejection, real or perceived. Medium; 2020. Available from: https://medium.com/@saint.drew/how-to-deal-with-cringe–4aed0d62836e

# ABOUT THE AUTHOR

**Shobha Nihalani** is an author, creative writing coach, and Mental Health First Aider. She has been writing for over 25 years and continues to follow her passion. In her youth, she lived in countries around Africa, Asia, North America and Europe, before settling down in marriage in Hong Kong. She started out as a freelance writer and journalist, but her dream was to write a book. Prioritizing family and domestic duties, she took her time to achieve her goal. In her early 40s, her debut novel, *Karmic Blues*, was translated and published in Denmark.

Now in her midlife, Shobha has 11 books under her belt and is recognized for her adventure and thriller novels: *The Silent Monument, NINE Trilogy, Unresolved, Trikon* and *The Blue Jade*. She has also written two non-fiction books: *Dada Vaswani: A Life in Spirituality* and *A Gift from Above: Haresh and Harini's Journey in Adoption*.

With the release of *Self-esteem in a Selfie World*, Shobha's passion is to help others develop their self-esteem and empower them to achieve their fullest potential.

www.ingramcontent.com/pod-product-compliance
Lightning Source LLC
Chambersburg PA
CBHW031105080526
**44587CB00011B/828**